My Darling Buffy

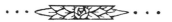

My Darling Buffy

THE EARLY LIFE OF
THE QUEEN MOTHER

Grania Forbes

RICHARD COHEN BOOKS · London

FRONT ENDPAPER: Back row, left to right: Alec, Fergus, Jock, Patrick, May, Rose
Front row, left to right: Michael, Elizabeth, Lord Strathmore, David on Lady Strathmore's lap

BACK ENDPAPER: The Duke and Duchess of York photographed after their wedding with
King George V and Queen Mary and the Earl and Countess of Strathmore

FRONTISPIECE: Elizabeth aged seven, with Peter her spaniel

British Library Cataloguing in Publication Data:
A catalogue record for this book is available from the British Library

Copyright ©1997 by Grania Forbes

ISBN 1 86066091 6

First published in Great Britain in 1997 by
Richard Cohen Books
7 Manchester Square
London W1M 5RE

1 3 5 7 9 8 6 4 2

The right of Grania Forbes to be identified as
the author of this work has been asserted by her in
accordance with the Copyright, Design and
Patents Act 1988

Designed by Margaret Fraser

Typeset in ITC Galliard by Banbury Pre-Press

Printed in Great Britain by
The Bath Press

For Edward, Matthew and George

Contents

There have been many books written about my great-aunt Her Majesty, Queen Elizabeth The Queen Mother, but none before has concentrated on her early life at Glamis before her marriage to Prince Albert. It was wonderful to discover that there was still so much about her in the castle archives and that the memories of those who knew her then remain so fresh.

The picture they paint is certainly a familiar one to me. Being in her company is always a delight because she makes everything such fun. I was her Page of Honour from 1970 to 1973 and one of my favourite expeditions was when she visited Dundee University as Chancellor. We used to travel north on the royal train, which was a great treat for a fourteen-year-old, and stop outside Edinburgh overnight. I remember one morning her private secretary Sir Martin Gilliat and I, dressed in all our finery, went for a walk along the railway tracks before breakfast. A train full of commuters passed the other way and the faces at the windows were a sight to behold. They could not believe their eyes.

Queen Elizabeth has always shown me great kindness ever since I was a small boy. I have vivid memories of going to tea with her at Royal Lodge when I was at preparatory school. We used to go for a walk in the icy cold and then come in to a feast. There were boiled eggs and toast dripping with butter, a wonderful feed-up for a schoolboy.

I also love going to stay with her at Birkhall where there is shooting and fishing and the most wonderful picnics. And it does not even matter if it rains because we put up a tent. It is enormous fun.

Queen Elizabeth, as the world knows, is a very special person and throughout my life she has meant a great deal to me. I am happy that this book, written in her honour, will be published for her ninety-seventh birthday and I hope those who read it will derive as much pleasure from it as I have.

Strathmore

Introduction

··· ⬥⧑⬥ ···

QUEEN ELIZABETH The Queen Mother is as old as the century. She was born while Queen Victoria was still alive, and whatever her position in society, her life would be of interest. She has the common touch. But in every other respect, The Queen Mother is uniquely uncommon. She was the youngest daughter of one of the oldest families in Scotland. She married into the grandest family in the kingdom. She has lived under five monarchs: six, if her brother-in-law who abdicated is included. She was the wife of one monarch, the mother of another and is the grandmother of the king-to-be. She has been at the heart of events that have shaped the modern history of Britain, and indeed has sometimes had a hand in shaping them.

When eventually The Queen Mother dies, there is no doubt that the nation will mourn her with more genuine sorrow and affection than any other person this century. She has a certain gritty determination that the British like to consider a national characteristic. However, her particular brand of doggedness is reassuring rather than intimidating. Throughout her long and often difficult life her bravery and resolution have been unfailingly accompanied by a cheery smile. Even when circumstances were at their bleakest – when her husband Bertie was unwillingly thrust on to the throne, when war came for the second time in her life, when she was widowed – the spirit and courage have scarcely faltered.

What is the source of such qualities? Perhaps the answer can be found in a closer study of her formative years, for Elizabeth Bowes Lyon enjoyed an exceptionally privileged and happy childhood, surrounded by a large and loving family. With insights provided by private papers that have never been made public before, interviews with contemporaries and relatives of The Queen Mother who have not spoken before, and photographs that have never been seen before, this book sets out to answer that question.

Elizabeth grew up amid the usual trappings of an aristocratic Edwardian household – nannies, tutors, pets, picnics, piano lessons and outings to the pantomime at Christmas. She was indulged by her family and adored by the servants. She became the most desirable debutante of her day. Chips Channon recorded in his famous diaries that she was 'mildly flirtatious in a very proper romantic old-fashioned Valentine sort of way... She makes every man feel chivalrous and gallant towards her.' 'I fell madly in love,' confessed one young man, all too aware that he was not alone. 'They all did.'

Yet despite her comfortable upbringing and the effortless popularity of her teenage years, the steel entered Elizabeth's backbone. Her eldest sister died before she was born, and an older brother when she was eleven. Another brother was killed in the First World War, and he was not the only one of her siblings to suffer in the trenches. When the family seat, Glamis Castle, was turned into a hospital for wounded servicemen, the fourteen-year-old Elizabeth learnt not only to care for ordinary soldiers with horrendous injuries but also to get on famously with them. Even during the worst moments, she could never shake off her natural vivacity and good humour for very long. In the midst of dressing soldiers' wounds and grieving for her own brothers, she remained an irrepressible teenager. Who else could have composed this limerick, found in the Glamis archives on the castle writing paper?

> The historic old castle of Glamis,
> Was peculiarly full of green palms,
> It is now full of soldiers,
> With bad wounded shoulders,
> And very bad heads, legs and arms.

In September 1916 a fire raged through the castle; Elizabeth led the fight against the flames and became a local heroine. Some of her family suffered misfortunes with spouses and children. One of them was possibly a murderer.

All these experiences contributed to her character but cannot fully explain it. A major factor was the stable background which gave her the self-assurance and stoicism needed to face the problems in the years to come. This was the young woman who, having hesitated before accepting the Duke of York's proposal, married him, helped cure his stammer, foresaw the abdication of her brother-in-law and prepared her husband for its inevitable outcome. It is no exaggeration to say that the crisis of 1936 placed in jeopardy the entire future of the British monarchy. The clear-sightedness of Elizabeth undoubtedly helped to avert catastrophe. She was every inch a king-maker.

An earlier biographer, Penelope Mortimer, ascribed her influence to sex appeal. 'It was her most formidable characteristic,' she writes. 'This doesn't mean that she invited anyone to bed. On the contrary. High moral principles, by inhibiting activity, produce an enormous reserve of sexual power. It was this power that transformed Bertie into a man of some stature, hypnotised the general public and eventually reinstated the throne in the public's fantasy.'

A modern interpretation would search in The Queen Mother's past for the grit that made the present-day pearl. This book reaches the conclusion that in some odd but heartening way it was the pearl that produced the grit.

I should add something about how I came to write *My Darling Buffy*. In 1995 I was asked to write a long, illustrated tribute to mark The Queen Mother's ninety-fifth birthday. Although I had been the Press Association's Court Correspondent for a decade, calling at Clarence House almost daily and watching her as she carried out her many engagements, I needed to do a great deal of new research in a brief space of time. To my delight, a number of her friends and family went out of their way to be helpful, among them the present Earl of Strathmore. It was Lord Strathmore himself who mentioned the room full of family archives at the top of the main tower at Glamis Castle. These records had never been explored by previous biographers of The Queen Mother, although there have been many.

Shortly afterwards, I took up Lord Strathmore's invitation to visit the archive. I toiled up the 143 steps of the spiral staircase, intending to spend a few days poking around: I ended up spending seven weeks in that dusty room. Here were letters and documents, old visitors' books and fading dance-cards that no one had seen for more than three-quarters of a century and that The Queen Mother herself had probably forgotten. That room at the top of the turret was the birth-place of this book.

As I worked on the archives, I came across other likely sources: old servants, members of the family, friends and relatives of friends. My account of the early years of Lady Elizabeth's life is based on stories handed down by the family, the recollections of tenants still living on the Glamis estate, the archives themselves and, of course, the work of previous biographers and historians. Among the papers in the tower I unearthed old schoolroom essays and school reports which even surprised The Queen Mother herself when she saw them again nearly ninety years later.

I met and interviewed Lady Mary Clayton, the daughter of Elizabeth's elder sister Rosie, who now lives in the grounds of Windsor Castle. She proved a spell-binding narrator. From her I learned about the family's belief that an American uncle poisoned two of her aunts, about the Bowes Lyon children's propensity for seeing ghosts and how the Earl of Strathmore liked to throw food at the countess during mealtimes.

In the chapter about the First World War, letters from members of the family and officers in the front line reveal the full extent of the grief and anxiety endured by Elizabeth and her parents. Here in detail is the story of how her brother Michael was lost, presumed dead, and then found again, after cashing a cheque in a German POW camp!

I discovered wonderful material in the unpublished diaries of Freddie Dalrymple-Hamilton, a Wodehousian figure who was devoted to Lady Elizabeth. I am grateful to Captain North Dalrymple-Hamilton for making his father's diaries available to me. Another rich source proved to be the racy private journals of Lady Rachel Cavendish. Lady Rachel married James Stuart, the handsome war hero whose romantic relationship with Lady Elizabeth is explored more thoroughly in this book than ever before. I spoke at length to James's daughter, the Hon. Davina Ritchie, and also to the daughter of his one-time fiancée, Evelyn Finlayson.

No previous biography has identified Prince Paul of Serbia as one of the most determined of Lady Elizabeth's many suitors. Through interviews with his son, who allowed me to see many of his father's letters, I became convinced that the prince had set his heart on making her his bride.

Mabel Monty, who was Lady Elizabeth's dresser and lady's-maid, proved a priceless source. She is now ninety-four but remembers the antics of her young mistress as clearly as though they happened yesterday. What is more, it transpired that she married a policeman who had played football as a lad with the young princes David and Bertie on the Sandringham estate

The illustrations for the book come from the private photograph albums of many of those involved in the story and from the Glamis archive itself, where I found many of them lying in old shoe-boxes. Lord Strathmore has given me exclusive permission for these pictures to be used, as have Prince Alexander of Yugoslavia, Evelyn Finlayson's daughter, James Stuart's daughter and the present Lord Gage.

Acknowledgements

· · · ❦ · · ·

My grateful thanks go first to Sir Alastair Aird, Queen Elizabeth The Queen Mother's private secretary, for his help and encouragement throughout the project; also to Sir Robert Fellowes, private secretary to Her Majesty The Queen, for his useful guidance, and to Major Nicholas Barne, private secretary to Princess Alice, Duchess of Gloucester.

I owe a special debt of gratitude to the Earl of Strathmore and Kinghorne and Mary, the Dowager Countess of Strathmore, whose kindness and knowledge throughout the writing of this book have been beyond price; also their archivist, Jane Anderson, who first showed me what she herself had discovered when she began sorting through material that had lain untouched for centuries. HRH Prince Alexander of Yugoslavia, Lady Mary Clayton, the Earl and Countess of Airlie, the Earl of Longford, Viscount Gage, Viscount Stuart of Findhorn, le Comte de Ribes, Lady Penn, Lady Clementine Beit, Lady Abel Smith, the Hon. Mrs Ritchie, the Hon. Mrs Jean Wills, the Hon. Mrs Osborne-King, the Hon. Mrs Margaret Rhodes, Captain North Dalrymple-Hamilton, Mrs Alice Winn, Mrs Cynthia Munro, Major Raymond Seymour, Neil Balfour, Oliver Everett, Mrs Mabel Stringer and Jock Scott have all given most generously of their time and their memories.

Early in 1996, when a publisher, having sat on the idea of this book for over three months, finally declined it, my six-year-old son George was aware of my disappointment. Twenty-four hours later he returned beaming from school. He put his arm round my shoulder and his cheek against mine and said, 'Don't worry, Mama, my friend Guy's Daddy is a publisher and Guy will make sure he publishes your book. We fixed it all in the playground, so you don't need to worry.'

Indeed he was right. Apart from Richard Cohen's faith in what was at first almost a Mission Impossible, so little being readily available, I was blessed with the outstanding team who worked such long hours to have the book ready in time for The Queen Mother's ninety-seventh birthday. Chief amongst them were Pat Chetwyn, RCB's managing editor, and Trevor Grove, whose wisdom and editorial assistance have made the book what it is. Margaret Fraser, the book's designer, worked equally hard, as did Christine Casley, its final editor. Thanks too in no small measure to my agent and friend, Clare Bristow, to Richard Mason, Mary Sandys and Christine Shuttleworth.

Finally, The Queen Mother was kind enough to read parts of the book at an early stage. Her pleasure at rediscovering long-forgotten memories was all I could have hoped.

· · · ❦ · · ·

CHAPTER ONE

Merry Mischief

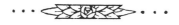

A THIN PLUME of smoke curling up through the broken slates of the brew-house had betrayed the guilty pair. Their mother was too relieved to be angry. The frantic, hour-long search of the house and grounds for her two youngest children had ended when one of the search party, passing the out-houses, smelt tobacco smoke. And there were the two small children, puffing away at an illicit cigarette.

They had discovered their secret den while hunting for bantam eggs and had called it the Flea House. It was in the attic of the ruined building where the household ale had once been brewed, up a rotten ladder – safe enough for small children but a death-trap for any grown-up.

'The attic was considered our very own parlour, though I must admit that a good many fleas intruded,' the little boy later recalled nostalgically. It became their 'blissful retreat' whenever they wanted to escape their morning lessons or hide from their nurse, Allah. 'In it we kept a regular store of forbidden delicacies acquired by devious means – apples, oranges, sugar, sweets, slabs of Chocolat Menier, matches and packets of Woodbines.'

The grubby little girl with the cheeky face and rumpled frock was Lady Elizabeth Bowes Lyon; her sidekick and co-tenant of the Flea House was her younger brother, the Hon. David.

Nearly a century later, it is difficult to imagine the nation's favourite grandmother as a conspicuously naughty little girl. Yet stories of 'the Imp', or 'Merry Mischief', as everyone knew her in her childhood years, are still remembered in the small Scottish village of Glamis and the Hertfordshire hamlet of St Paul's Walden Bury, where she grew up – and where the episode of the Flea House took place.

Much later she would be 'Buffy' to a small circle of her nearest and

'The Imp' - Elizabeth aged two in furry coat and hat

1

dearest. But in those early days Lady Elizabeth's nicknames derived from her endearing if sometimes exasperating love of fun. The earliest biography of Elizabeth Bowes Lyon, written by Lady Cynthia Asquith and long out of print, remains the only source of early childhood stories. Lady Cynthia vividly remembers one of young Elizabeth's favourite pranks, known as 'repelling raiders'. Visitors to Glamis Castle would arrive at the main door for tea with the Imp's mother, Lady Strathmore – the ladies in their finest frocks and ostrich feather hats, the gentlemen in their Sunday best – only to find themselves deluged by cascades of cold water from above. This 'boiling oil' was tipped on the intruders by Elizabeth and David, manning the castle's topmost tower. As the startled guests mopped themselves down and gazed aloft, muffled giggling would be heard from behind the parapet ninety feet up.

On another occasion the old coachman, apprehensive of driving the newly-acquired automobile, was ambushed by the two children who managed to smuggle an old football under one of the car's front wheels. Lord and Lady Strathmore emerged innocently from the castle and waved goodbye to their grinning offspring, solemnly settling into the soft leather of the car's rear seats. Solicitous footmen laid fur-lined rugs over their knees and shut the doors. The order was given to proceed and the novice chauffeur, adjusting his goggles and holding the steering wheel in a vice-like grip, engaged the clutch. A resounding explosion ensued.

The shaken man was helped from the driving seat and the vehicle inspected. It was quite clear who was responsible but, long before the echoes of the report had died down, the culprits had completely vanished.

The six-year-old Elizabeth was not merely a mischievous but a remarkably knowing child. One day she could not resist the lure of taking a pair of scissors to a new set of sheets, which she gleefully cut to ribbons. She was asked what her mother would think about this. 'All Mother will say,' she replied confidently, 'is "Oh! Elizabeth!"' And she was right.

In the early part of this century, the Bowes Lyons formed a large, close-knit and strong willed family. Elizabeth was the ninth of the ten children born to Claude and Cecilia Bowes Lyon. Her father, who became the fourteenth Earl of Strathmore in 1904, came from an even larger family, consisting of twelve brothers and sisters. Her mother was one of the three daughters of the Rev. Charles Cavendish-Bentinck, a cousin of the Duke of Portland, and Caroline Louisa Burnaby.

Mr Cavendish-Bentinck died six years after his marriage, and five years later his widow married Harry Warren Scott, the third son of Sir William Scott of Ancrum. Widowed again in 1889, Caroline Scott thenceforth divided her time between England and her home in Italy at the Villa Capponi, overlooking the city of Florence, which was to become the scene of some of her granddaughter Elizabeth's happiest childhood memories.

When Elizabeth was born, on 4 August 1900, Violet, the eldest of her brothers and sisters, had already died, of heart problems brought on by diphtheria. The next in line was Mary, always known as May, who was then seventeen. After May, the order went: Patrick (Lord Glamis), Jock, Alec, Fergus, Rosie and Mickie, who was seven years older than Elizabeth. When she was twenty-one months old, her younger brother David arrived to complete the family.

Although it has always been denied that the countess's youngest children were spoilt, their older brothers and sisters often complained that the 'two Benjamins', as they were known, 'got away with murder'. This is hardly surprising given that Elizabeth and David were so much younger than the rest of their enormous family.

Lady Strathmore (or, more accurately, Lady Glamis: the earldom had not yet passed to Elizabeth's father, although to avoid confusion this narrative will mainly refer to her family by its later, grander title) was thirty-eight when Elizabeth was born and forty when David came along.

Although she was still a very handsome woman, she used to remark wryly that she was often mistaken for their grandmother. Her youngest daughter's birth seems to have caused hardly a ripple at the time. Elizabeth's grandfather does not even mention it in his diary entry for 4 August 1900 and makes no reference to her in the weeks that followed, nor does any correspondence survive detailing the events of that day.

This means that the recent controversy about her exact place of birth has been difficult to resolve. It was accepted that Lady Elizabeth was born at the family's Hertfordshire home, The Bury. Her birth certificate, filed at the register office in Hitchin by her father, clearly states her birthplace as St Paul's Walden Bury, and for most of her life no one had any reason to doubt it. The Queen Mother herself unveiled a plaque in the local church, All Saints, commemorating the event. However, shortly before her eightieth birthday, she suddenly announced that she had in fact been born in London.

Since then authors and historians have expended a good deal of energy wrangling over the mystery. Passport Number 380040, issued

Lady Strathmore; a miniature
painted c.1908 when she
was forty-six

Lord Strathmore c.1895

Violet who died at the age of
fourteen from heart problems
caused by diphtheria.
A painting by Mabel Hankey,
foremost miniaturist of
the day

OPPOSITE: The earliest
surviving photograph of
Elizabeth. The chair can still
be seen at Glamis.

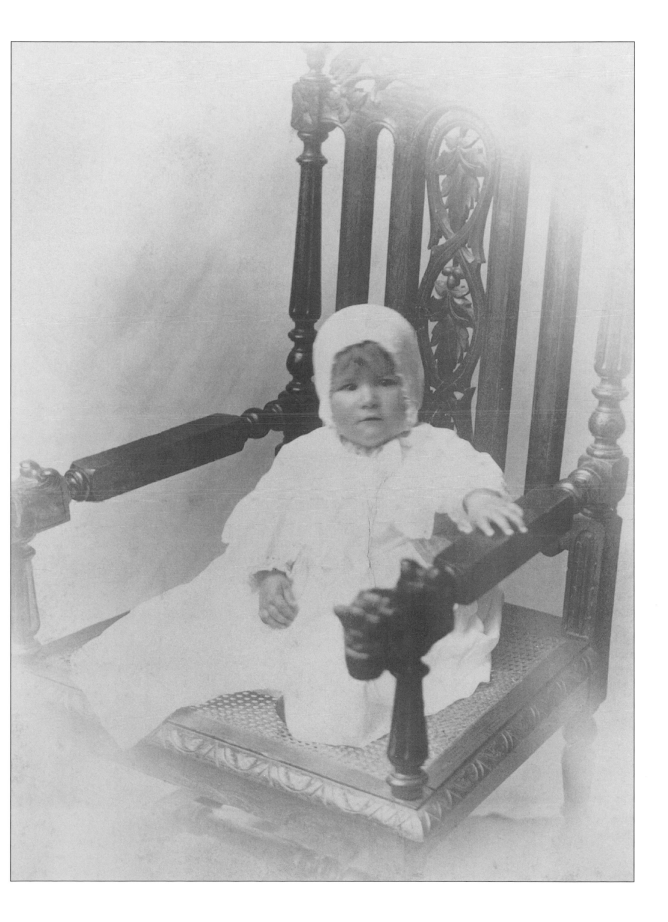

by the Foreign Office on 23 May 1921 to Lady Elizabeth Angela Bowes Lyon and signed by Lord Curzon himself, might be thought to have put an end to the matter. Under 'Description of Bearer' it reads: 'Age:20; Height: five feet two inches; Forehead: normal; Eyes: blue; Nose: normal; Mouth: normal; Chin: round; Hair: dark brown; Complexion: fresh; Face: round; Peculiarities: none; National status: British born subject.' And in the slot allocated for place and date of birth, it states: 'London, 4th of August, 1900'. But The Queen Mother has refused to be drawn further. 'It is of no matter,' is all she will say.

Canon Dendle French, for many years vicar of All Saints church in St Paul's Walden Bury and now private chaplain to Lord Strathmore at Glamis, has his own theories. When The Queen Mother made her surprising announcement in 1980, he travelled to Falmouth in Cornwall to find the daughter of the Rev. Tristan Valentine, who was vicar at St Paul's Walden Bury at the time of Lady Elizabeth's birth. Margaret Valentine, then aged ninety-one, told him she had been playing the piano in the vicarage parlour when a maid came over from The Bury and announced that Lady Glamis, as Elizabeth's mother was then titled, had had a baby.

The following week, on his way home, Canon French called on a Berkshire man with whom he had earlier corresponded. He was told that the man's father-in-law had been a local general practitioner in Welwyn and had always asserted that he was present at Lady Elizabeth's birth. He went on to say that the doctor had actually been invited to her marriage to the Duke of York.

'If she were born in London, then why on earth did they send for a provincial doctor?' asks Canon French. 'It does not make sense.'

His third strand of evidence comes from a local woman, Elsie East, whom he knew through the church at St Paul's Walden Bury. Elsie East's aunt used to do all the laundry for the Bowes Lyon family when they were in residence at The Bury. She told Elsie that Elizabeth was definitely born at St Paul's and recalled what a mess there had been.

It is difficult to resolve these conflicting clues. One theory is that Lady Elizabeth was actually born in a London hospital but taken to her waiting cradle at St Paul's when she was a few hours old. This is not altogether implausible: by the time the countess was pregnant with Elizabeth she was nearly thirty-nine and had already borne eight children, the last of them, Michael, a whole seven years earlier. Her doctors might well have advocated caution and advised that delivery take place in a hospital, with specialists on hand should the need arise.

However, having a baby in hospital was not considered altogether acceptable in those days, surprising though that seems today. It is possible that in such a case a veil would be drawn over the actual place and circumstances of the birth. Which of course would account for Lord Strathmore's minor aberration when he registered his daughter.

Another intriguing theory suggests that Lady Strathmore went into labour unexpectedly as she motored from her London home in St James's Square up to Hertfordshire passing Welwyn *en route*. As this was her ninth child, and considering her age, the impending birth would have been an emergency with no time to lose. Perhaps a local GP was summoned – the very man mentioned to Canon French – and Lady Elizabeth Bowes Lyon, our future Queen Mother, was actually born at the side of the road.

If so, the doctor would have been anxious to get the countess and her new-born baby home as quickly as possible. And there could indeed have been something of a mess after she had been put to bed at The Bury, just as the laundry maid said. If such were the case, Margaret Valentine, interrupted at her piano playing to be told the news of the birth, would naturally have assumed that the delivery had taken place at the house.

One further possibility is that the absent-minded Lord Strathmore simply made a mistake. He was six weeks late in recording his daughter's birth and the notification did not reach the proper office until two days before Lady Elizabeth's christening. Men in those days, and certainly men of Lord Strathmore's rank, were not over-concerned about childbirth, and in the case of the earl, a degree of forgetfulness about the details of his daughter's arrival would have been especially unremarkable.

Those who knew him well describe him as a vague and somewhat eccentric man. His customary dress was an old mackintosh tied with a piece of twine. He spent much of his time digging ditches and doing chores in the grounds and was always much amused when visitors mistook him for one of his own labourers.

Jock Scott, whose father was tenant at the Mains Farm in Glamis, is now ninety years old and retains vivid boyhood memories of the earl:

> I can see him now, busy brushing away the snow. Three gardeners were standing round with their arms folded, just watching him. He was a very fit man and would do any job on the estate. He loved the outdoor life. He would take an active part in whatever was going on and was never afraid to get his hands dirty. He took a special interest in the rhododendrons and was often to be seen cutting them back in a vigorous fashion.

One particular habit baffled them all:

> On moonlit nights, he would summon his valet, Mair, in the early hours of the morning and walk into the woods to lop dead branches off trees. The pair of them would then drag the branches back to the castle and lug them to Lord Strathmore's study. There the earl would chop them up for kindling on the hearth. It's nobody's business how many hearths he destroyed that way. When he was asked why he chose that particular hour of the night to collect wood, he would reply with a smile, 'It's the only time I get any peace.'

He was prepared to tackle any job he asked another man to do and he was a generous and considerate laird even when his finances were at risk. 'The Strathmores were not a rich family like some others,' says Mr Scott.

> They sometimes had to sell off land to make ends meet and it was local knowledge that whenever we heard shooting, we knew there was a party planned up at the castle. They needed the game for the dinner table.
>
> But however hard up he was and however lazy or incompetent the man, the earl would never lay off or sack one of his workers. He would rather do the job properly himself. He knew what a sacking would mean to their families. That is why he was such a grand man and a good Laird to work for. He was a very devout Christian but not the sort who goes to church three times on Sundays and then comes out and fires a man. He put his religion into practice and looked after his neighbour, whoever that might be. He was a quiet, kindly country gentleman.

Despite his rank, the earl was far from stuffy, and enjoyed a whisky and a good party:

> He was not one for standing on ceremony and often used to come up to the Mains to see my father, who was a good pal of his. They would sink a good few drams and the earl was quite the life and soul of the party – away from the watchful eye of Her Ladyship, you see.
>
> He had a good sense of fun and loved jokes and telling stories. One of his favourites was how he had met a visitor in the drive when the Dundee folk had been invited to Glamis for their annual picnic. Quite a few of the men used to bring a bottle of whisky with them to help the day pass off well and two of them happened to spot him as he was pollarding a tree. It was a perishing day and, of course, he was dressed in his normal fashion. One of them approached him and said, 'You poor man. Fancy the earl making you work in weather like this'. Handing the laird his bottle, the visitor added, 'Here take a swig of this to warm you up.' The earl obliged and the man went off none the wiser. Lord Strathmore would never have thought of embarrassing the visitor by letting on who he was. That's the sort of man he was. But he didn't mind telling the story afterwards to make folk laugh.

Lord Strathmore was also fond of recounting the tale of how he had received a furious letter from a minister of the Kirk complaining that it was a 'scandal' that he made his labourers work on the Sabbath. In fact the man whom the minister had seen clearing out a storm-drain on that Sunday afternoon had been the earl himself, doing what he considered to be a little light gardening. A courteous letter was sent to the outraged cleric nevertheless, with a suitable apology from the laird and a promise never to allow 'such a despicable act' to happen again.

Lady Elizabeth's mother, formerly Cecilia Cavendish-Bentinck, was entirely different. A vicar's daughter, she was related to the Dukes of Portland and had inherited the strength of character that marked her family. She was the dominant personality in the home and all her children adored her. Even when they were grown-up and married they still turned to her for help and advice. As one of her friends remarked, 'If there is a genius for motherhood, she has it.'

However, though loving, she was not lax and expected the highest standards from her children. She was a true Victorian, much given to the stern maxims found on the carefully worked samplers of the period. 'Work is the rent you pay for life,' was one of her favourites, while another declared: 'Life is for living and working at. If anything or anyone bores you, then the fault is in yourself.'

In photographs Lady Strathmore appears an elegant, handsome woman with strong features, beautiful eyes and an aquiline nose. According to a former housemaid she usually dressed in black because 'she always seemed to be in mourning for someone'. Mrs Mabel Stringer, who worked for the Strathmores for a number of years, recalls that 'she always wore the most wonderful clothes: silks and brocades. You could hear her rustling as she approached. And her hats – well, they were the talk of the county. She was a beautiful, stately woman and a kind, if exacting, mistress.'

The countess was a strong-willed woman who disregarded much of the fashionable dogma of the time. Unlike most women of her rank and upbringing, she insisted on breast feeding all her babies, ignoring the convention that a wet nurse should be employed. So Elizabeth spent the first eighteen months of her life sleeping in a cradle at her mother's bedside.

A nanny, however, was essential. When Elizabeth was a month old, Lady Strathmore employed Clara Cooper Knight to look after her, which she did for the next eleven years. Always known as 'Allah', since that was the closest the children could get to pronouncing her name, she was the daughter of a tenant farmer on one of the Strathmore estates. Allah was strict but kindly: a quiet, sturdy, utterly dependable woman of the highest principles, she presided over the nursery at The Bury with rock-like devotion.

Allah served the Strathmore family for generations. She went on to look after Lady Elizabeth's nephews and nieces, before being poached back to look after her original charge's own daughter, our present Queen. Never one to compliment lightly, she remembered Elizabeth as 'an exceptionally happy, easy baby; crawling early, running at thirteen months and speaking very young.'

Lady Strathmore's mother formed a similar impression. In August 1903 she wrote to her daughter in somewhat mangled English: 'Elizabeth beaming in every way. Is she not advanced for three? Sometimes she might be six. You must certainly treat her as Lady de Vasci did Mary and that, through the advice of doctors and professors, let her do NO LESSONS till she's eight!' The countess naturally ignored her mother's counsel.

For the first few years of her life, Lady Elizabeth lived at The Bury. She has fond memories of the big, rambling Queen Anne house, covered in magnolia and honeysuckle, set in the rolling Hertfordshire downs. It was warm and comfortable, if a little shabby, with the lived-in look of a family home. A protective gate, surrounded by scrapbook screens made by older brothers and sisters, marked the entrance to the children's quarters. It led into the nursery, with its battered toys, scuffed skirting boards and a large brass fender in front of the fireplace on which wet shoes could be dried. Pictures illustrating favourite children's stories, which had been hung by the estate gardener as long ago as 1880, still decorated the nursery walls. Beneath them were recorded the heights of previous occupants. The room was redolent of cosy afternoons by the fire, toasting crumpets and roasting chestnuts.

However, it was the wood, with its ponds and lake and hidden statues, that was Elizabeth's special delight. She was convinced it was the haunt of fairies. There she spent happy summer afternoons sitting in the shadow of the big oak tree reading a favourite book, with her two ring-doves, Caroline-Curley-Love and Rhoda-Wrigley-Worm, beside her in a wicker cage. If the weather were fine, tea was taken outside, usually beside the statue the children had christened the Running Footman or Bounding Butler, but more correctly known at the Discus Thrower.

Elizabeth and David were keen on funerals. Whenever they found a dead bird, which was often, it had to be given a solemn burial. The corpse would be interred in a small wooden box lined

10

Watercolour of Elizabeth
c.1906, also by Mabel Hankey

The 'two Benjamins' with the
garden at St Paul's in the
background

with rose-petals. The children made up their own service, of interminable length and complexity, which they intoned together before the coffin was finally laid to rest.

Elizabeth had a less morbid relationship with her hens. As a child she would get up early every day to feed them, and to make sure that no ravening fox had broken in during the night. There were dogs and Persian cats and tortoises in her menagerie; but the favourite was her little Shetland pony, Bobs, who followed Elizabeth everywhere, even into the house and up the staircase.

There were also two splendid pigs which the children regarded as pets, black Berkshires named Emma and Lucifer. One day to their horror they discovered that Lucifer was gone. They rushed to the house to report the theft, only to discover that he had been despatched to the local fête as a raffle prize. Elizabeth was determined to win him back. The children broke open their money boxes and begged what extra cash they could. They then set about buying every raffle ticket they were able to lay their hands on. They did their best, but before long their funds ran out and they managed to secure only half of them. It was not enough. Despite their gallant efforts, Lucifer was won by a stranger and they never saw him again. It was a long time before Elizabeth and David could forgive this wicked betrayal.

Much as she loved The Bury with its assorted pets, the sorties to the wood and the Flea House, the fun of helping with the haymaking (which Elizabeth described as 'getting very hot in a delicious smell'), The Queen Mother has told her relations that her first memory comes from Scotland. She says she can recall sitting on her grandfather's knee in the drawing-room at Glamis and looking out of the window to watch the fairy lights on the lawn.

The occasion was the thirteenth earl's golden wedding on 28 September 1903 when Elizabeth had just turned three. The whole family was invited to join in the festivities which went on for four days. According to the earl's diary, the grandchildren presented him 'with a lovely grandfather clock, with a brass plate listing their twenty-seven names written on the dial'.

What Elizabeth particularly remembers is the third day, when 'some 600 guests from a five-mile radius of the estate were entertained to a garden party, tea and pipes'. A cinematograph entertainment followed the bagpiping, showing what was then regarded as the height of sophisticated screen entertainment: 'many pictures of numerous characters'. Later reels were danced to the accompaniment of Mr Neil and his String Quartet. 'The whole park was lit in the evening by Chinese lanterns and padella lights,' wrote Elizabeth's grandfather.

Even at that time, Glamis made a strong impression on the future Queen and throughout her life she has greatly prized her Scottish heritage. In her youth she discarded her more English surname of Bowes completely and called herself simply Elizabeth Lyon.

Mr Stratton, the local minister, noticed this trait in her as a little girl, when she paid visits to the manse:

> She was particularly fascinated by my portrait of Prince Charles Edward Stuart and always went up to it and gazed at it. I have a note from her, written at a very early age, in which she asks if she and her governess can come to see my 'objay d'art'. She was particularly fond of coming to see my collection of family relics and curios and showed a wonderful knowledge of these things for so little a child. She also wanted very much to go down to the burial vault of her ancestors, but I drew the line at that.

A rather more girlish passion than exploring her lineage was the pursuit of delicious contraband from behind the green baize door. On one occasion at Glamis she had been taking tea with visitors upstairs, making polite conversation, but as the maid withdrew with the tea things Elizabeth pursued her downstairs. She knocked at the door of the still-room, where such delicacies were kept, and memorably enquired, 'May I come in and eat more – much more of that chocolate cake that I liked to eat while it was upstairs?'

Sometimes the children's approach to the still-room and pantry staff was more demanding. Elizabeth and her little brother were in the habit of begging for pennies to buy sweets. 'May I have silver pennies this time?' she once asked unabashedly. Presumably they were confident of being indulged, although this didn't stop Elizabeth from playing the young madam and admonishing the servants if she felt they were ignoring the rules of good housekeeping. 'If you could make the pats of butter a little smaller, it would be much better. Persons leave some of the big pats on their plates and that is very waste,' she told them.

The housekeeper at Glamis Castle was not immune to their charm, declaring them 'the dearest little couple you have ever seen':

> Lady Elizabeth always took the lead. She would come tripping down the stairs and it would be, 'Mrs Thompson, have you any of those nice creams left for us?' and she would open the cupboard and help herself to what she liked best. I can see her now coming outside the window of the housekeeper's room with her pony, Bobs, and making him beg for sugar. Often she would come up by herself and pop her head up suddenly to make us all jump. She thought it a great joke. She and her brother were like two little imps dancing about.

As a little girl, Elizabeth was enthusiastic about her dolls – but they

On the steps of the castle: a rare photograph of the whole family together.
Back row, left to right: Alec, Fergus, Jock, Patrick, May, Rose
Front row, left to right: Michael, Elizabeth, Lord Strathmore, David on Lady Strathmore's lap

'Merry Mischief' and David paddling in a burn on the moors near Glamis

OPPOSITE: Elizabeth had an early love of horses and learned to ride when only three

14

had to have eyes that opened and shut and hair that could stand vigorous brushing. It wasn't long, however, before she turned to more adventurous pastimes. 'She was a proper little tomboy,' recalls Jock Scott.

> She did everything her brothers would do. She was forever up a tree, climbing far too high and giving her mother heart failure. She was very daring.
>
> She loved anything on four legs and had lots of pets – dogs, rabbits, guinea pigs and cats. She spent hours fussing them and was desperately upset when any of them died. She was a good horsewoman but with her you could only go at one speed – full pelt. You often saw her in her red riding habit tearing round the estate. She would get back to the stables, flushed and excited and full of derring-do. Her pony would be flecked with sweat and she would help the groom to rub him down, talking away the whole time. She was a great chatterbox. She loved her ponies and always had a lump of sugar in her pocket for them. She was full of fun and mischief. Not at all stuck up. She had a good word for everybody and mixed in with the common folk.

Cowboys and Indians was a favourite game. Lady Elizabeth and the Hon. David would spend hours in the woods collecting feathers to make head-dresses and plastering their faces in paint, before sallying forth to raid the village. Those on the Glamis estate today remember their grandparents' stories of being ambushed and tied to trees or fence-posts until a 'ransom' had been paid. A regular target was the dairy. Armed to the teeth, the pair would sneak up by the wood and burst through the door and, with blood-curdling cries and threats of scalping, extort a drink of milk and a biscuit.

The Benjamins were always on the look-out for mischief. One day, stalking the grounds, they spotted a labourer up a long ladder painting the castle windows. On the ground below he had left a large, open tin of white paint. As he worked away, Elizabeth and David crept up, took a spare brush and painted all the lower rungs of the ladder. Watching from a safe distance, they were thrilled to see the man descend the ladder and walk white footprints all over the immaculate green lawn.

On wet days Elizabeth loved dressing up, choosing her outfit from a wonderful treasure-chest full of costumes and wigs. She and David would make up plays and put on performances for the grown-ups. She adored being the centre of attention in a large party of adults and often contrived to be invited to the dining-room, persuading her mother that an unlucky thirteen would be sitting round the table if she were not included. A former butler remembers asking Lady

16

Strathmore, 'How many will be taking luncheon today, Your Ladyship?' Quick as a flash, Lady Elizabeth replied, 'Fourteen, if you count I.'

For all her impudence, the young Elizabeth was full of precocious charm and quick to learn the social graces. Visitors remember her, still at the stage of having to bring both feet in turn on to the same stair, busily conducting them upstairs to show them to their rooms. At the age of three she was discovered by her mother pouring tea, for which she had rung herself, and making small talk to a party of neighbours who had arrived early.

On another occasion, she turned to a distinguished guest and enquired 'Shall us sit and talk?' She then led the surprised gentleman away from the rest of the party to an alcove adjoining the drawing-room and addressed him earnestly for fully three-quarters of an hour. When another friend of her parents asked teasingly whether she were yet engaged. 'No, not yet,' she answered. 'It was only Mother what gave me this ring.'

She bumped into the factor in the village one day and greeted him thus: 'How do you do, Mr Ralston? I haven't seen you look so well, not for years and years, but I am sure you will be sorry to know that Lord Strathmore has got the toothache.' Gavin Ralston worked on the Glamis estate for forty-five years and the Benjamins often used to go to tea with him and his sister.

One day, their nurse noticed that the children were missing and rushed out to find them. A gardener had been pruning the fruit trees which still grow up an eighteen-foot wall that borders the house, and had left a ladder propped against it. The pair had climbed up the ladder, and to their nurse's horror were seen running along the top of the wall. They were coaxed down, but Lady Elizabeth later confessed, 'My goodness, we were soundly smacked when we got home.'

Her natural sense of tact sometimes let her down. On one occasion a great friend of the Strathmores, Lady Nina Balfour, had come to stay at St James's Square. As she arrived, David remarked to his sister, 'We haven't had no presents lately, Elizabeth.' To which the latter replied in a ringing voice, 'No, but perhaps we shall get some big ones now Nina has come to London.'

Elizabeth was a strong-willed child and prepared to have a thoroughly good fight with anyone, be it her 'darling bruver' David or even Mother. Her parents' great friend Lord David Cecil says that the siblings, while devoted to each other, 'used at times to quarrel furiously, using hands and teeth on each other with all their youthful vigour.' And a former housemaid recalls that when mother and

David in jester's costume and Elizabeth in pink brocade and silver dress copied from a painting by Velasquez. These were their dancing costumes in which, to their disgust, Lady Strathmore made them perform for the benefit of the grown-ups

daughter had a set-to Lady Strathmore would exclaim, 'I feel very sorry for the young man you marry, Elizabeth, because you are so determined.'

One source of friction was that Mother liked her two youngest children to dance a minuet when she gave an entertainment at Glamis. Although keen enough to star in productions of their own devising, they found the exacting nature of this sort of performance in front of such a large audience daunting. However, despite the tantrums, the countess generally prevailed. Elizabeth would be laced into a long pink and silver brocade dress, made by her mother and copied from a Velasquez painting. David wore the pride of the dressing-up box, a jester's costume complete with cap and bells. The Strathmores had been the last family in Scotland to employ a jester.

The minister at Glamis went to one such entertainment and noted that 'for one brief, yet supreme, half-hour the Seventeenth and Twentieth Centuries were one ... When suddenly the music stopped and the little dancers, making a low bow and curtsey, clapped their hands with delight. Little choruses of praise were heard on every side and Lady Elizabeth, when I asked her the name of the character she had adopted, said with great *empressement*, "I call myself The Princess Elizabeth."'

CHAPTER TWO

Brothers, sisters and ghosts

· · · ❧ · · ·

THE HISTORY of the Bowes Lyon family abounds with colourful characters, but none is more mysterious than Mr Augustus Edward Jessup, Elizabeth's 'wicked Uncle Gus'.

The archive at Glamis contains a photograph of Augustus Edward Jessup, of Philadelphia, USA, and his bride Mildred Bowes Lyon, second daughter of the thirteenth Earl of Strathmore, taken on their wedding day, 1 July 1890. They received a total of 700 presents but few to match those given by Mr Jessup himself to his bride. These included 'a diamond rivière and tiara, a pearl and sapphire necklace, a turquoise and pearl necklace, a topaz and pearl necklace, a silver casket of Italian design, a silver Elizabethan pocket watch and an Indian necklace of five strands of rubies, sapphires, emeralds and moonstones.' Mr. Jessup was out to impress.

The family, however, soon began to have reservations. Lady Mary Clayton, the daughter of Elizabeth's sister Rose, remembers being told:

> At parties, he always had a pretty nurse standing beside him with a bowl of water and towels. After shaking hands with each guest, he would wash his hands before moving on to the next one.

Mr Jessup was clearly a very strange man, but it was more than that. Within seven years of marrying him, Mildred was dead. Although they were unable to prove it, the family later suspected that she had been poisoned. Lady Mary takes up the story:

> First of all Uncle Gus married my grandfather's sister and killed her after two little boys were born. They were brought up by Lord Strathmore's youngest sister, Maudie, and since their father had run through all their mother's fortune she decided to send them to grammar schools because she knew they hadn't the money to live the life of aristocrats.

The Strathmore family tree, as designed by Rose.
Top to bottom:
Lady Strathmore, May, Patrick, Alec, Lord Strathmore, Jock, Rose, Fergus, Elizabeth, Michael, David

The wedding in 1890 of Augustus Jessup ('wicked' Uncle Gus) and Mildred Bowes Lyon. He later married Lady Strathmore's sister, Cynthia Cavendish-Bentinck. Did he poison them both?

Then to everyone's dismay Gus married my grandmother's sister, Cynthia. They had two daughters and then she died. The family always thought that he had poisoned her too, killed her as they gadded about Europe. The little girls were brought up by their maiden aunt, Violet Cavendish-Bentinck, in Italy.

The family's suspicions about Uncle Gus are reinforced in letters written by Mrs Scott to her eldest daughter, Lady Strathmore, during Cynthia's lifetime. In November 1911, she wrote, 'Do you ever hear anything cheering of poor Cinty? I often feel sad for her. She is very discreet but ... one feels she must mind her life dreadfully. To me it is unbearable. It must be next to impossible not to despise Gus but I suppose it is an illness and only a hair's breadth from insanity.'

By July 1915 Cynthia's situation had evidently deteriorated:

Gus has written to say that Cinty has been very ill again – that he wired for Dr Goodbody who says she is not in immediate danger and that they are coming to England very soon but that she is needing most skilled care.

22

What does that mean C. darling? I feel so worried and so angry with Gus.
   If Cinty was so ill, was it right of him to tell us nothing till after Goodbody had had the time to come – isn't it strange his not telling us what's wrong – I feel so bothered and yet, I believe it's half of it not true – I don't feel an atom of trust in a lot he says.

Another letter from Mrs Scott to Cecilia discusses her determination to change her will so that in the event of her death Gus will not benefit.

Lady Mary Clayton says the story had a sad ending, as though it were not grim enough already. 'In the First War, the boys joined the Merchant Navy and both were killed. It was the greatest shame because my mother told me that they were both exceptionally nice. The little girls disappeared and no one knows what happened to them.'

If the family's suspicions about 'wicked Uncle Gus' were even partly true, it is almost impossible to understand how he got away with it. The question remains: how much is fact and how much family hearsay? We shall never know.

Lady Mary is an absolute goldmine of such family stories. She is a splendid old lady, now eighty, living with her husband in a grace-and-favour cottage in Windsor Great Park. The walls of her cosy house are covered with photographs and paintings of the family, including a fine portrait of her mother. Dominating the sitting-room is an impressive bronze bust of her father, sculpted by Lady Mary herself before failing eyesight forced her to give up an artistic career. Visiting her is like stepping back in time. She talks lucidly and tirelessly in the authentic tones of Edwardian England. But her greatest merit as a raconteuse is that Rosie was obviously the kind of parent who did not leave her children's upbringing entirely in Nanny's hands but enjoyed being with them and relished handing down the spiciest family sagas. Lady Mary has an endless fund of such stories, another of which concerns one of Elizabeth's uncles who became a diplomat and met an untimely end. 'He was serving in Poland and got killed in a drunken race against a train. His horse put his foot in a rabbit hole and threw him against a tree and that was the end of him.'

The story did not end there. This uncle's wife, 'a stupid French woman who treated her children very badly', decided to return to England by sea:

> She had her three daughters with her, as well as her eldest son and her baby boy, who was in his nanny's arms. They were shipwrecked. The girls and the baby were saved but the boy was drowned. The three girls, who were contemporaries of my mother, were very beautiful and led vivid lives. Sadly the baby boy turned out badly.

Maude Bowes Lyon, Lord Strathmore's youngest sister, who never married and who brought up her sister Mildred's two sons. Lady Mary Clayton remembers her as 'witty and fun and a wonderful violinist'

23

I don't think their father was a wrong'un. It was just that their mother was rather vague and hopeless and didn't know how to look after them. If she had had money to get someone else to care for them, they would have been all right.

Examples of such bizarre behaviour abounded in Elizabeth's family. The fourteenth earl, her father, was himself notably eccentric. The thirteenth earl had been famous for adapting Gilbert and Sullivan operas for his twelve children to perform in the dining-room at Glamis. But his son was happier declaiming than singing. According to Lady Mary Clayton, Claude 'preferred to quote endlessly from the *Ingoldsby Legends* and *Alice Through the Looking Glass.*'

She remembers he also had unusual views about eggs.

Long before anyone else, he thought eggs were deadly poisonous and avoided them at all costs. If he watched you eating a boiled egg at breakfast, he would shake his head sadly and say, 'Poison, my dear. Poison, my dear!'

He was very agile, even in his eighties, and used to go out to clean up his trees. For some reason he was also fond of boiling up leeks which he used to feed to his grandchildren. They were full of grit and horrid.

Lord Strathmore was a fanatical cricketer and matches at Glamis were taken very seriously. In a memoir, Lord Gorell describes tense moments on the pitch:

In a match against Brechin, the castle side had eight runs to win and six wickets in hand: Uncle Pat, Lord Strathmore's brother, who was out, even then refused to be confident of victory until we all declared that if we were beaten he would be justified in his pessimism for ever – and we actually lost by four runs!

Yet another year, Brechin, always our most dour opponents, won by one wicket, the last run being daringly obtained off a catch in the slips – dropped of course in the tension! There was always incident and excitement in plenty over cricket at Glamis: once we all subscribed for a Panama hat for our captain, Lord Strathmore, in honour of his doing the 'hat-trick' against the Dundee Drapers.

Lord Strathmore's interests were by no means exclusively sporting. He used to do the *Daily Telegraph* crossword and read the Bible every day and was extremely devout. His father had nearly bankrupted the estate by building Episcopalian churches all over Scotland. 'My poor grandfather inherited an absolute load of debts which he had to spend his life paying off,' says Lady Mary:

The Strathmores were not well off but, unlike most lairds, they were exempt from a tax called the Jacobite Passage because, most fortunately, at the time of the 1745 rebellion, the Lord Strathmore of the day was a

The Bury, St Paul's Walden
Bury, the Strathmores' home
in Hertfordshire

Left to right: Jock, Patrick,
Lord Strathmore, Michael,
Fergus and Alec in 1901 –
David was to follow in 1902

Rose at the piano, with Fergus
and May singing. Their mother
was a talented musician and
wanted all her children to learn
an instrument.

RIGHT: Picnic on the grouse
moors. 'Buffy' is third from the
left. The animated figure on
the right is Lady Christian
Dawson-Damer, Fergus's wife

ABOVE RIGHT: Glamis Castle,
the Strathmores' family home
for 500 years

FAR RIGHT: Lord Strathmore,
'a fanatical cricketer', bowling
during the Glamis v. Brechin
cricket match of 12 August
1908

minor and so did not take part. Also they weren't madly keen on the Stuarts because King James V of Scotland had had poor Lady Glamis burnt at the stake. After that they no longer served the crown which was just as well.

Lord Strathmore was a kindly and indulgent man, but on occasion he could put his foot down. Lady Mary remembers:

> his youngest brother Malcolm asking if his wife could come to stay. We were all rather anti his wife. She was very pretty and rather useless and poor Malcolm had been rather jockeyed into marrying her by his Colonel for some reason, at the end of his time in the regiment.
>
> My grandfather just patted him gently on the hand and said, 'No Malcolm, not this year' and that was the end of that. Nothing more could be said. It was after my grandmother had died otherwise she would have heaved a private sigh and said, 'Yes, of course'.

Lord Strathmore was also in the habit of 'bowling' food at his wife. Elizabeth's niece Jean Wills remembers him lobbing Christmas pudding down the length of the huge dining-room table; Lady Mary recalls oranges flying through the air. The countess, however, seems to have been more than a match for her husband, deftly fielding whatever he bowled at her. 'She never muffed it,' says Lady Mary. 'Then he used to come round and sit on the corner of her chair and put his arm round her. It was very sweet. They were very devoted.'

Lady Strathmore had a tremendous zest for life and her enthusiasms were infectious. She was the driving force behind many a scheme and under her influence all her children developed a confident and uninhibited approach to life, very much in her own style.

It was she who spent nearly a decade planning and executing the Italian garden at Glamis which is still one of the glories of the estate today. Two acres of shrubberies were cleared and the whole area enclosed by high yew hedges. Within these hedges, in ten concealed alcoves, she placed statues of her children. Patently she loved them quite as much as they loved her. A plaque, dated 1910, and bearing the names of all those who participated in the work, marks the completion of the grand enterprise. The Italian garden may well have nourished Elizabeth's own burgeoning interest in gardening, which remains a passion to this day.

As the châtelaine of three very grand houses, Lady Strathmore was practical and efficient. Her meticulous account books still survive, with every household expenditure, to the last bar of coal tar soap, noted down. Wherever possible she used produce from the estate, keeping butcher's bills to the minimum. Yet she was not stingy with her servants. Her former housemaid Mabel Stringer remembers that half a sheep would often be served in the butler's dining hall: no one ever left the table feeling anything but completely satisfied.

Lady Strathmore was a brilliant hostess and renowned for her wonderful parties. She had an easy-going manner with a talent for making even the shyest guest blossom. Her daughter inherited this skill, always able to make the person she is talking to feel the most important in the room. At the dinner-table Lady Strathmore sparkled, dispensing warmth and laughter. Wherever she was, her homes in Scotland and England were always full of visitors. She took pride in her cooks, the most celebrated of whom, Mrs MacClean, she had trained herself. 'Mrs MacClean's cooking was really a work of art,' says Lady Mary. 'But when anyone praised her, she would reply that it was all my grandmother's doing. She had just been a little girl from the village and my grandmother taught her all she knew.'

One of Lady Strathmore's cooks was particularly temperamental. He was last seen rushing out of the family's home in St James's Square brandishing a huge kitchen knife, running down the pavement in pursuit of the kitchen boy. 'I don't think either was ever heard of again,' Lady Mary recalls.

In the few quiet moments available to her, the countess would withdraw to her private sitting-room. This was called the Tapestry Room for she enjoyed working in petit point and was very skilled at what was known as drawn-string work, an art which she taught Mrs Stringer, who later passed it on to Lady Elizabeth. However, her principal form of relaxation was playing the piano. 'The lasting memory that I will have of her,' recalls a frequent visitor to Glamis,

> is seeing her, her face a picture of concentration, bathed in a pool of candlelight sitting at the piano in the drawing-room. The rest of the room was in semi-darkness and the glow of the fire was reflected off mirrors and silver picture frames.
>
> She was very gifted and played with great emotion. She was heard in complete silence and it was an experience that no one could help but find moving.

Lady Strathmore often invited distinguished musicians to stay when she was entertaining. Huge dinner parties would be followed by a private concert, performed by the family and their guests, with the piano and violin as the favourite instruments. The younger children, who should of course have been in bed by this time, found their own way of joining in these entertainments. There was a trap-door in one of the bedrooms at Glamis which led, via a tiny stone staircase set in the thickness of the wall, to the drawing-room. So when these concerts took place the children were able to creep down and, putting cushions on the cold steps, sit smoking cigarettes and eavesdropping on the performance. 'I suppose they knew we were there but they never minded. I think they thought it quite good for us to listen to the music,' remembers Lady Mary.

The secret stairway was just one of the features that made Glamis so mysterious and exciting in the eyes of its younger occupants. The oldest inhabited castle in Scotland, Glamis is wreathed in legend. In its grounds lies St Fergus's Well, whose magical properties for centuries made it an object of pilgrimage. More than 600 years ago, when the castle was to be built, the site had to be moved because, it was said, the 'imps' used constantly to remove the foundations. It is widely believed that Glamis was where Macbeth murdered King Duncan and where King Malcolm died of his wounds following a battle on High Hill. The bloodstained stones which supposedly bear witness to this event are there to this day, covered by a wooden floor.

Elizabeth and her siblings delighted in terrifying new visitors to the castle with chilling tales about its history. The most persistent and certainly the spookiest of the many legends is that of the Monster of Glamis. All the evidence suggests that the 'monster' did in fact exist. Throughout Victorian and Edwardian times there were whispers that somewhere in the Strathmores' recent past lurked a horrible and shameful secret which took the shape of a grotesquely misshapen creature, hidden within the castle. Descriptions of its appearance differed. One suggests that the creature had an immense chest, 'hairy as a doormat ... His head ran straight into his shoulders and his arms and legs were toy-like.'

During his research into the mystery, the historian Paul Bloomfield came to the conclusion that the 'monster' was none other than Thomas, eldest son of the eleventhth Earl of Strathmore and his wife Charlotte, whom he had married in December 1820. According to *Burke's Peerage*, she bore their first child, a son christened Thomas George, on 22 September 1822. However, Douglas's *Scots Peerage* says that Charlotte and her husband had another baby, also called Thomas, 'a son born and died on October 21, 1821'. Cockayne's *Complete Peerage* and Debrett also record the birth and death of this first son, but give the date as 18 October.

Mr Bloomfield deduces from this that the son and heir born in October 1821 was hideously deformed: the story is that the infant was not merely hairy, but egg-shaped. His parents must have decided to record him dead, since it was clearly unthinkable that this baby should inherit the title and estates. In any case, they probably assumed that the child would not live beyond a few days but, according to Bloomfield, 'he lived and he lived'. Local legend relates that the rightful heir was mewed up in a secret chamber built inside the castle's charter house by the first Earl of Strathmore in the 1680s. Here, it is said, the 'monster' spent many sad years in solitary confinement, his existence known only to a select few.

His younger brother, the second Thomas, was presumably initiated into the secret when he came of age, as would have been his brother Claude, Elizabeth's grandfather. However, when her own father reached his twenty-first birthday, on 14 March 1876, it seems that he was not required to view the 'monster' in his cell. Possibly he was dead by then, although the precise date of his death will never be known. According to Elizabeth's sister Rosie, who heard it from Fairweather, the head gamekeeper at Glamis, a workman who saw something alive in a secret room in 1865 was 'subsidised and induced to emigrate'.

Mr Bloomfield states:

It is thought that the monster was well cared for during his lifetime. He probably never left the castle and, never having known liberty, did not miss it. Equally probably, he was exercised on the leads of the roof at night, hence the name 'The Mad Earl's Walk' still given to a part of the roof. He may once have escaped and been recaptured. That would account for the legend told me by Sir David Bowes Lyon, Lady Elizabeth's younger brother, of 'Jack-the-Runner' racing across the park in the moonlight.

Gavin Ralston, the fourth generation of factors to have served the Strathmore family, was once asked by Lady Strathmore for the full, true story of the monster. According to journalist James Wentworth-Day, who researched the whole story for an article in the *Daily Telegraph Magazine*, Mr Ralston looked at her gravely and slowly shook his head before replying, 'Lady Strathmore, it is fortunate you do not know it and will never know it, for if you did you would never be happy.'

Wentworth-Day goes on:

Ralston was a hard-headed, dour man, greatly respected and no person to be easily scared. Once he was dining with Lord and Lady Strathmore on a winter's night when the ground was already snowbound. It snowed again, heavily. Soon the park was four foot deep in snow and Ralston lived almost a mile away. 'You can't possibly go home in this,' said Lord Strathmore as they sat after dinner in front of a great fire. 'Stay the night. there's a bed ready for you.' Ralston refused point-blank. Nothing would induce him to spend the night in the castle. Instead, he got every gardener and stableman on the place out of bed to dig a path through the snow to his home.

Wentworth-Day also interviewed Rosie about the monster. 'She looked serious and was silent for a moment. Then she said, "We were never allowed to talk about it when we were children. Our parents forbade us ever to discuss the matter or ask any questions about it. My father and grandfather refused absolutely to discuss it."'

Elizabeth's nephew, Timothy, Lord Strathmore, was also unable to shed much light on the matter. 'The legend may have died with my father, or with my brother who was killed in the last war. I feel there is a corpse or a coffin bricked up somewhere in the walls. They are immensely thick. You could search for a week and find nothing.'

According to Lady Mary Clayton, the family were used to living with such presences:

> David used to see ghosts. My mother took him for a walk at Glamis when quite a little boy, about five or six, and he said, 'Look. Look at that man running down the drive,' and of course my mother looked and there was nobody there. He said he had seen a man dressed in seventeenth-century clothes running messages.
>
> The Grey Lady was seen by Aunt May. Aunt May was always late, very unpunctual. Granny could never get her to be there on time so she was always in a rush going downstairs to dinner. She noticed this person on the landing outside her room and she thought she must be a new housekeeper. She asked her mother about it one day and they both suddenly realised that she had seen a ghost.

Lady Rachel Cavendish, fourth daughter of the Duke of Devonshire and a great friend of Elizabeth, kept a witty private journal which she referred to as 'Rachel's Ramblings'. A frequent visitor to Glamis, she recalls being told about the castle's ghosts:

> I had heard a lot about it from various people and about 'Beardie' and ghosts and things but to stay there that first time was great fun and no spooky feeling at all.
>
> I was told that if I did hear odd noises in the night, it would only be 'Father cutting up wood'. It appears he was a bad sleeper and split up logs in his bedroom to pass the time. I once went into his room by mistake, when we were playing sardines, and there at the bottom of his bed was an axe and a huge pile of logs ready to be cut up the next night. The split ones were removed by Barson the butler and a fresh pile put there every day.

The Beardie referred to by Lady Rachel was a former heir to the Strathmore title whose ghost was supposed to haunt the castle. One night Beardie had carried on playing dice into the early hours of following day which happened to be the Sabbath. Reminded that midnight was about to strike, he is said to have roared, 'I care not what day of the week it be. If we have a mind to, we shall play on until Doomsday.' The devil then appeared, to announce that the miscreant's own doomsday had indeed arrived. In consequence of his wrong-doing, he is said never to rest at peace and still to be seen sitting by a great fire in one of the bedrooms, a huge old man with a flowing white beard.

Lady Rachel recalls one of her earlier visits to Glamis:

> I remember Mike Lyon saying that one room was Beardie's and that the floor sloped. Years later I stayed there but had to arrive the day before James, my husband, and Lady Strathmore said, 'I am sorry to put you in this room but will move you when James comes tomorrow'. I couldn't think why as it seemed a very nice, rather Victorian room; but when I went to bed, I dropped a ring and it rolled right into the corner. Then I remembered about the room with the sloping floor.

Lady Mary remembers her mother, Rosie, telling her about seeing a ghost – though not at Glamis:

> It was in the house in St James's Square. On one occasion she and one of her brothers had come down from Glamis and had stopped at the house before catching the train down to St Paul's Walden Bury. She leant over the banisters to shout to her brother about the luggage. Something caught her eye and she turned round and looked up the passage. She saw a totally strange young man in spongebag trousers looking up the passage at her. She drew herself up to her full five foot two and said 'What do you want?' in an icy tone. As she was about to speak again, she saw the Georgian door-handle beginning to glimmer through his body and then he was gone.

On another occasion Rosie was sitting reading in her mother's sitting-room when her spaniel and Fergus's collie both suddenly jumped up and 'pointed' to the corner of the room. They then started to retreat howling. 'It was all too much for my mother. She rushed out of the room in terror, closely followed by the dogs,' says Lady Mary.

She is convinced that both Rosie and David were fey and had some kind of sixth sense about the supernatural.

> My mother was the one who always looked after people and I feel certain that she had the gift of healing. People naturally seemed to get better when she was looking after them.
>
> Also, my mother's dreams used to come true. She was once staying with my grandmother, Mrs Scott, in Italy when she dreamt that the bishop would call in his carriage and invite her to go on an expedition; then they would stop and she would pick some lily of the valley. She thought

nothing of it until the following day, when exactly what she had dreamt came to pass.

It was Rosie who, after the war, was sent for to look after Patrick, Lord Glamis, the eldest of Elizabeth's brothers. He had served with the Scots Guards and luckily escaped serious injury. However, he was very badly shell shocked. 'I don't think he ever got over it,' says his niece.

> It was really the start of his Faustian ruin because he was just beginning to make a success of his life again as a parliamentary candidate for the Durham area when his wife Dorothy said she couldn't bear to live up there any longer.
>
> Dorothy insisted that they had to move south to East Grinstead. So his political career came to nothing. Then they started a coal export business with the Germans and of course when the Second World War came, the whole thing collapsed.

Dorothy, the daughter of the Duke of Leeds, was not the most popular of the Strathmore family relations. When she became engaged to Patrick, Lady Strathmore's mother, Mrs Scott, observed that the Leeds family were 'as poor as church mice' and so not much of a dowry would be forthcoming. The Duchess of Leeds herself wrote to Lady Strathmore three days before the wedding saying that in all honesty she did not consider Dorothy a suitable wife for anybody. She was certainly not an ideal mother: one of the reasons she antagonised the rest of the family was her extraordinary treatment of her eldest son, John. Eventually Lady Strathmore became so concerned that she decided she had to rescue the boy. Lady Mary recalls the story as told to her by Rose:

> What happened was that when she was still quite young my mother went to stay with them at the lovely family house in Durham. In the evening the little girl, Tida, and Cecilia, who was a baby, would be brought down by their nanny to play with their mother in front of the fire. Poor John would be sent over to the cold end of the room to play with telephone directories.
>
> My mother used to go over and play with him, which annoyed Dorothy very much. Rosie told this to her mother when she got to Glamis and my grandmother went down and took him away and brought him up like a younger son. My mother said Dorothy's attitude was partly due to a very bad birth and partly to a horrid nurse who used to leave the baby for two and a half hours on Dorothy's bed in the afternoons when she was still recovering from the birth. Of course, he used to scream his head off and I suppose, despite nature, that made her take against him. He turned out to be the most beautiful child. He was the best looking young man I have ever, ever seen.

34

Tea-time for Elizabeth's nephews and nieces at St Paul's. It was they who christened her 'Buffy'. Behind them is the statue of 'the Discus Thrower', which Elizabeth nicknamed 'the Running Footman'

'Buffy' with Patrick, his wife Dorothy and son John. Elizabeth's feelings for her sister-in-law can be gauged by the distance between them

However, John was killed in the Second World War. 'It was all very sad for Pat, my uncle, because he was the gentlest of creatures. He was so good looking and amusing and quite unaware of it. He was very tall and looked like a Greek god, with marvellous classical features.'

After Patrick and his family moved south, Lord Strathmore was forced to remove the roof of the old house in Durham because he could not afford to pay the rates. It is now derelict, although the Strathmore family still go shooting at Streatlam, putting up at another house nearby.

Jock, fourteen years older than Elizabeth, was the next brother in line. He married the splendidly-named Hon. Fenella Hepburn Stuart-Forbes-Trefusis. Sadly their first child Patricia died as a baby, of acidosis, for which there was then no cure. This was in 1917, while Jock was serving at the British Embassy in Washington.

Typically thinking only of his wife, he wrote to his mother, 'It was a terribly sudden blow for poor Fenella but she has so far stood it very well ... The baby is buried in Rocks Creek Cemetery – a very pretty place under tall trees. Fenella, I am glad to say, the doctor had managed to keep away from the funeral. We had a little service in the house first.' He goes on to say that they had tried to get a doctor from Baltimore who was the greatest authority on the condition, but only managed to contact him after 'all was over'. Even if the illness had been diagnosed twenty-four hours earlier, said the doctor, 'no treatment would have saved baby's life. It is a truly dreadful thing.'

Further tragedy was to strike the family. Jock's wife's family carried a congenital defect which prevented two of his four surviving daughters from developing mentally. According to Lady Mary:

> They were missing one vital nerve that connects the two halves of the brain, which meant that they could not grow up normally. They were incredibly beautiful little things and very sweet. We all used to play together and we were the greatest of friends. You couldn't help liking them. We all used to go out to the park together and it was like trying to tame some little wild creature in the woods. They couldn't speak, but they were very sensitive and responsive to you. Jock was a darling and adored all his children. Despite this sadness he was always very lively and amusing.

The next brother was Alexander. He died tragically of a brain tumour when he was only twenty-four years old, after he was hit on the head by a cricket ball. 'He must have had unbelievable charm,' says Lady Mary, 'because his fellow clerks kept his job open for him by doing his work for over a year, until he died. He was working for an insurance firm in the City. The family knew he had a brain tumour but in those days it was inoperable.'

Until his final illness Alec, as he was always known, had been as lively as the rest of his brothers. According to Lord Gorell, a close friend of the Strathmore family at that time, 'wonderful dressings-up were devised in the evenings, as when Alec in charades brought the house down as the "great gulf fixed between Heaven and Hell".'

The Bowes Lyon children seem to have been involved in a constant round of family games or mounting impromptu entertainments. Lord Gorell describes a typical occasion:

Lady May's birthday came at the end of August, and that was hailed by her brothers as an opportunity for comic speech-making, Jock replying on her behalf with sallies that called for her amused indignation, and Fergus for the ladies, to the laughter of all – after which Elizabeth, sitting up late in honour of the occasion, would consent very sleepily to be taken to bed.

Fergus was the next-born of Elizabeth's brothers and, according to Lady Mary, quite different from the rest of the Strathmore boys:

He took after the Cavendish-Bentinck or Wellesley side of the family and showed great promise as a soldier. He would have gone far if he had not been killed in the First World War.

He served in India and once bribed one of his bearers not to die. The man, for some reason, had threatened to do so and when Indians say they are going to die, they jolly well do die. Fergus produced a sovereign from his pocket and said to the man, 'If you don't die, I will give you this' and the chap decided against it.

In a letter written to his brother Michael in August 1912 from Fort William, Calcutta, Fergus says wistfully:

I suppose you are now slaying the wily grouse in myriads, making thousands of runs and generally enjoying yourself! This is a beastly hot place, as I have often told you before. There is so much fever here that two companies (mine one of them) have been stopped going out for Field Training next week ... Who has been staying at Glamis? Any nice people? Write and give me some particulars. Are you lording it over everyone? I don't think, not arf. I hear the partridges are rotten, which is bad luck – especially after a record year like last year was. Can't get my leave to go off and try for tiger, however I think I may be able to get a week or 10 days at Christmas.

Fergus was a keen naturalist, to whom the countryside was always a source of wonder. 'My mother said that when you went for a walk with him, he would suddenly stop and point and say "Look". And you would look and see nothing. Then he would put down his hand

OPPOSITE: Rose aged about fifteen. She was always regarded as the beauty of the family, and was much admired by the Prince of Wales

Rose's daughter Mary, now Lady Mary Clayton. She was banned from being Elizabeth's bridesmaid by her mother on the grounds she would be too naughty

Michael drawn by Rose in 1912. It is one of only two of her drawings that survive

and bring up a rabbit in his palm. It was like magic,' says Lady Mary. 'That's why he married Christian Dawson-Damer. They were both mad about bird-watching and had a shared interest in country matters.'

Fergus did not share his brothers' passion for cricket although once, according to Lord Gorell, 'a match at Arbroath depended entirely on the ability of Fergus, a great wag as well as a dear and gallant fellow, but no cricketer, to achieve the unusual and make a run, and amidst cheers for once he managed a fluke shot.'

Michael, or Mickie, seven years her elder, was Elizabeth's favourite brother. He became high-shouldered and asthmatic from the privations he suffered as a prisoner of war. The diary he kept as a POW and letters home show that the men were practically starved by their German captors and had to rely on food parcels from home to stay alive.

Mickie hoped for a career in the City, but his delicate health forced him to become a pheasant farmer instead. The entire Strathmore family were famously charming, but he and his younger sister Elizabeth were devastatingly so. 'I remember David telling me that he had never known anyone like Mickie. Anyone whom he talked to, even a brief word with a total stranger, went away feeling that Mickie was his friend for life,' says Lady Mary.

Surprisingly, he was one of the last of the brothers to marry, but he finally settled down with Elizabeth's friend, Betty Cator, a handsome and generous woman who 'could whistle any tune like an angel'.

Rosie, three years his senior, was Mickie's great companion yet, like all children, they sometimes squabbled. As Rosie's daughter recalls:

They used to remind each other of the time when he threw a knife at her and it quivered into a tree just behind her head. He used to respond by saying that she had nearly drowned him when he was trying to get back into a punt after bathing in the pond. He was tilting the boat as he was trying to get in, and so she banged his fingers with the punt pole.

However, Lady Mary describes another occasion from their early childhood, when Rosie saved Mickie's life:

She was in a little pebbled cave at the end of the pond reading a book when she heard thump, thump, thump, crash and splosh. He had been climbing up the back of the Georgian grotto and had slipped on the layered roof, banged his head and dropped unconscious into the pond.

Rosie managed with great difficulty to pull him out, but thought it rather odd that he should go to sleep there and then. Luckily the vicar's wife was walking past on her way to see my grandmother. She saw Mickie

was unconscious, picked him up and took him back to the house. If he had been on his own, he would have drowned.

David was Lord Strathmore's youngest son and Elizabeth's lifelong companion. He and she were the 'two imps'. One only has to look at his smile to know that he was, in the words of a former housemaid, a tearaway – and would probably remain one even as an adult.

His nieces, Jean and Margaret Elphinstone, remember him well. 'Uncle David was wonderful and wild. He was full of laughter and fun. He always played with us and to go off with him was the greatest excitement. It never mattered what we did, it was always heaps of fun.'

Elizabeth also joined in and Jean remembers the occasion when, together, they sneaked out mattresses and slept on the stone steps in front of the castle's great entrance. 'Elizabeth helped us to organise it,' remembers Jean. 'We were bitten to death by midges and got up at 5a.m. We then went to the kitchen garden and ate all the goose-berries.'

When David was sent off to Eton he missed Elizabeth intensely, writing to 'Darling Buffy' whenever he could. 'Thank you so much for your letter,' he wrote plaintively on one occasion. 'I loved it especially as nobody but mother will write to me so far. I feel as if I have been here years and years . . .'

The letter goes on to enquire about his washing and some new suiting before adding:

> Do you know if Father has been reading any of my numerous letters lately as I have been sending him daily epistles which will soon be supplemented by telegrams. Read that to him out loud preferably while he is sucking or biting his cocoa. Then at the end he will say 'What, my darling?' and you will read it again and he will then say 'Bars' and wipe his moustache with a napkin that has already been used at breakfast and is lying in some neighbouring chair. He will then say, 'I am much too busy at present, darling.' And trot out of the dining-room with his unlaced boots and then sit doing nothing at his cigarette table till he remembers the Davelyou [Strathmore-speak for lavatory], where curiously enough I am now going to.

In another letter home, this time to his mother, David describes how the Eton boys reacted to the announcement that peace had been declared:

> I write in bed after one of my happiest days! Isn't it too marvellous to be true that we heard this morning at 12.15 when the headmaster read out a telegram from The King stating: Hostilities ceased at eleven etc. etc.
> Eton on the spot went completely mad. There was a general rush for

flags and in half an hour very nearly every Etonian was bedecked in flags and waving them. For the next hour and a half like insurgents we paraded the streets, cheering everything and everybody; making a colossal row with a band, the instruments varying from gongs, bugles to hip-baths and hammers. The founder in the school yard was decked with flags and every house was literally covered with flags and colours. It was a wonderful sight and never have I seen a happier throng.

According to David one Eton master – 'Basil Johnston by name' – tried to put up three red flags but these were pulled down and he was 'kicked' away.

Rosie's daughter remembers her mother telling her that David used to suffer from appalling headaches:

Nanny liked to go to farm dances and my mother was left in charge of the two younger children. She told me how she used to have to walk David up and down the nursery because he cried from pain as soon as she put him down.

When he was old enough to go into business he was told he couldn't. He would have to live a quiet life. Being David that wasn't good enough for him so he went as an ordinary gardener to Kew and worked there for about eighteen months and was so much better. At the end of it, he was able to go back and be a very successful businessman. He was a merchant banker at Morgan Grenfell.

Mary – May to her family – was the eldest of the Strathmore children, seventeen years older than Elizabeth. She inherited her mother's auburn hair and golden eyes and was the tallest of the girls. She also inherited her mother's strong sense of duty. Her daughters remember her as strict, but kind and generous and much given to helping those less fortunte than herself. Also like her mother, May was a wonderful gardener.

'She was brought up to take her responsibilities in life,' says her daughter Margaret:

After she was married she used to work every day in the slums of Edinburgh at one of the first shelters to look after mistreated children. My mother was very devout and had an immense sense of duty. Those poor children came from the most terrible homes and she was determined that she would help them in any way she could. I remember my sister and I picking primroses to sell in aid of her work – great bunches of them.

Mary Clayton says: 'I think all the brothers and sisters had great fun and their German and French governesses had a pretty thin time as they were ragged to death. The one exception was Aunt May. They used to say "Don't tell May. She will tell mother."' She was certainly the kindest and gentlest of creatures. Her daughters remember that as

41

a little girl Elizabeth used to climb into bed with May and her husband while they were drinking their early morning tea.

Rosie was a completely different character. The favourite and the beauty of the family, she was much admired by the Prince of Wales (later King Edward VIII). Lady Strathmore gave up trying to match-make after Rosie turned down her twentieth proposal of marriage. She eventually married the man of her choice, William Spencer Leveson-Gower, a young naval officer always known as Wisp. Lord Granville, as he later became, eventually rose to be a rear-admiral, a post of which his wife was exceptionally proud.

Blue-eyed and golden-haired, Rosie was exceptionally attractive. She was witty and fun and nobody was better at telling a story, a joke, a titbit of gossip or some choice piece of ancestral tittle-tattle. As a teenager she was also the one who looked after 'the little ones', Elizabeth and David. This could sometimes be an alarming responsibility, as her daughter recalls:

> One day Rosie took Elizabeth for a walk when she was thirteen and Elizabeth was three. She took her in the afternoon for a little wander along the bird path towards the wishing well. Halfway there, a great big young tramp suddenly got up from the undergrowth and approached them.
>
> My mother was terrified and he made her promise to bring food and money that evening. She took Elizabeth by the hand and walked slowly round the corner and then she ran as hard as she could back to the castle. She didn't tell anybody. That shows a difference between children of that era and children of today. She was terrified that this man would appear and find them in the evening. Nothing happened. But I suppose it never occurred to him to lay a finger on them. Those days were far more innocent.

Her daughter describes Rosie as a fearless rider and a daredevil on the hunting field. 'She had no idea of trotting or jumping. She just went through a hedge. She had a lovely Arab pony, given to her by her youngest uncle Malcolm, who fought in the Boer War.' Oddly enough, Elizabeth, unlike her elder sister, was much less keen on riding than the household servants remembered. Their accounts of Elizabeth galloping around on Bobs are contradicted by Lady Mary, who says: 'Aunt Elizabeth had two horrid ponies that frightened the life out of her and she has never liked riding since.'

As Lady Mary's father was in the Navy, the family led an unsettled life and she did not meet her Aunt Elizabeth until she was six:

> I vividly remember the first time I saw her which must have been a day or two before her wedding. My brother and I were seated in a taxi either side

of our nanny, outside Bruton Street. The door opened suddenly and this delicious young girl popped her head in and said 'Hello Mary! Hello Baba' and vanished. Apparently I was invited by Elizabeth to be one of her bridesmaids but my mother said 'No', so then my cousin Anne was asked. Years later, I felt very envious of Anne. If she could do it, so could I. I was four. It would have been a tremendous responsibilty and my mother was anxious since I was always the naughty one - rather like Aunt Elizabeth!

If Elizabeth was naughty as a young child, she was to become even naughtier as a schoolgirl.

CHAPTER THREE

Willingly to school

$\cdots$ ❦ $\cdots$

ELIZABETH'S education began almost as soon as she could talk. Patiently taught by Allah, she learnt her alphabet from the faded pictures around the nursery walls at The Bury. As the fire crackled in the grate on winter evenings, Elizabeth laboriously repeated her ABC and traced copper-plate handwriting into a lined exercise book. The dotted outlines proved awkward at first: there were occasional tantrums. Allah, as ever, was firm – though not above offering the occasional prize of a small piece of chocolate.

'Allah was quite strict but very, very loving,' recalls one of her later charges, the Hon. Jean Wills. Mrs Wills is a niece of The Queen Mother, the daughter of Elizabeth's sister May, and is now a tiny, bird-like lady in her late eighties living in a splendid Georgian house full of flowers. She is not much younger than Elizabeth and remembers her as being a particularly jolly aunt who kept pet pigs, played games and danced congas when they were all children. She inherited her Aunt Elizabeth's nurse and was under her care for fifteen years. She has fond recollections of what life was like under Allah's benevolent tutelage.

'I remember in the nursery, on Sundays, if we had been good, we were given Rob's Rusks which we were allowed to dip into weak, milky tea. It was the greatest luxury – our Sunday treat.' However, if little Jean Elphinstone, as she then was, had not behaved herself retribution was swift:

> I used to be quite clever at hiding food I didn't like such as fatty bits of bacon and suchlike up my sleeve or in my apron pocket. Of course it made my clothes very greasy and smelly and I was always caught out. Allah used to get very, very cross about that.
>
> We used to go downstairs after tea to play with our parents and I

From her earliest years Elizabeth had the precious ability to look relaxed and informal in front of the camera. This shot was taken at Glamis c. 1908

45

remember my horror when Allah appeared at the door unexpectedly early and said I was to go upstairs to bed ahead of my little brother. My parents obviously asked why and she told them, as I blushed hotly. I don't think I ever did that again.

All the same, the Elphinstone children loved Allah dearly. 'We were terribly upset when she left to look after Princess Elizabeth.'

Lady Strathmore herself undertook the task of teaching her younger children to read and write, starting with Bible stories. By the time David and his sister were six and seven, they could give a fairly detailed account of the highlights of the Old and New Testaments, from the Creation to the life of Moses and beyond.

Elizabeth quickly learnt to read, and obviously enjoyed books. 'I remember that she devoured books, lying on her tummy, with elbows propped against the hard floorboard,' recalls one of the servants at The Bury. 'She would lie there for hours on end completely engrossed. Her elbows would be rubbed red raw.'

Her taste was as catholic as most children's. Early on, books about animals were special favourites, particularly if they involved Shetland ponies like her own beloved Bobs. Then came adventure stories, handed down from her older brothers and sisters.

Elizabeth loved fairy stories, not only reading them but writing her own. An unfinished manuscript in her childish handwriting shows a lively, if somewhat derivative, narrative style. Here, published for the first time, is the unabridged, unedited text:

> There was a very big forrest were a very poor family lived. There was Mr Peak, Mrs Peak and two children. the hut was very small and in the room were they had there meals there was two wooden chairs and a bench and a hard wooden table.
>
> Well as it happens they were eating there meal and they heard a knock at the door. Mrs Peak went to open the door. There was quite a young man. He came in and asked if he could warm himself as it was so cold outside. He took one of the chairs and sat down and looked about him to see what was around him. He thought at first that he might stay for the night but seeing how poor they were he went away.
>
> 'Well I wonder who he is,' said Mrs Peak. 'He looked very much like a prince but it wouldn't do to think so Mother.' Mrs Peak gave no arurnser. We must go to bed now, goodnight, goodnight.'
>
> So they all went and lay on thier hard matrices.
>
> Capter two
>
> The run into the woods
>
> Next morning Joan and Fred as the two children were called went out for a walk into the forest. They went further till they came to a little open

He thought at first that he might stay for the night but seeing how poor they were he went away.

Well I wonder who he is said Mr Peak he looked very much like a prince but he wasnt do you think so Mother

Mrs Peak gave no answer We must go to bed now goodnight goodnight.

So they all went and lay on thier hard matrises.——

Chapter two.

The run into the woods

Next morning Joan and Fred as the two children were called, went out for a walk into the forest They went further till they came to a little open space where to their horror the saw an enormous dragon four heads and and a slimy neck with crimson rings all over its mouth

space were to their horror the saw an enormous dragon with four heads and a slimy neck with crimson rings all over its . . .

And there the reader is left in suspense.

Elizabeth was entranced by tales of chivalry, her imagination fired by the romance of knights in armour, damsels in distress, tournaments and quests. Even more to her taste were sagas from her family's native Scotland, with their mixture of magic and reality. From these early enthusiasms evolved a strong interest in history that has stayed with the Queen Mother throughout her life. Geography, too, she found exciting, poring over atlases and no doubt dreaming of travelling to foreign lands. Certainly there was nothing insular about Lady Strathmore's attitude to 'abroad'. From the age of six, Elizabeth and David had a series of French (and later German) governesses. Mademoiselle Lang was the first. She was a great disappointment to the children because she was no good at cricket. But Mademoiselle Lang must have been a good teacher, for by the time Elizabeth was ten she spoke French almost as readily as English.

Art was not her strongest subject. Unlike her elder sister Rosie, who could draw with real skill, Elizabeth's efforts left much to be desired. Somehow the finished effects looked peculiar, her human figures notable for their elongated bodies and huge noses. Yet she appears not to have been deterred by her lack of talent, doodling away energetically even in the margins of essays.

Despite the evidence of unpromising material, Lady Strathmore, was ambitious for her daughter's artistic education. She employed Thornton Andrews, a professional artist with a studio in Chelsea, to take Elizabeth in hand. It seems that, like her grandson Prince Charles, landscapes were her preferred subject. In August 1916 Mr Andrews wrote to Elizabeth's mother concerning holiday homework: 'I am sending herewith my account for the lessons to Lady Elizabeth. I am pleased to think that she will have ample subjects at Glamis for trying her hand at sketching out of doors.' He added:

> I should advise her not to attempt a view of the whole castle at once lest it should be too difficult and she should become discouraged – but rather confine herself to a small portion – say one of the towers, sitting just so far off as to get the top of the tower within an angle of 30 degrees in line of sight.
>
> Perhaps you would be kind enough to explain this to her; and also to remind her what a nice effect may be got by just shading rather emphatically with a soft pencil, then spraying – and then tinting with thick flat washes of colour.

Elizabeth drawn by Rose (who found her nose difficult). From her earliest years she loved reading

Whether Elizabeth followed these instructions is unknown. None of her efforts, whether sketched, sprayed or tinted, has survived. The only artistic endeavours of hers that exist are the screens and scrap-books she and her brother assembled, as did so many children of that generation. On wet days she and David would set to with scissors and paste, leaving the nursery knee-deep in cut-up Christmas cards and butchered magazines. Their efforts provide a haphazard record of popular images of the day, which inevitably included a great many pictures of animals.

Elizabeth evidently continued to enjoy this kind of collage-making for there is an example of what might be called her maturer work at Glamis. It is to be found in a lavatory at the top of the Red Staircase. Elizabeth covered its walls with contemporary cut-outs, including a great many Punch cartoons, which are still there to this day.

Schooling the Bowes Lyon children in the social graces was as important as their academic education. Music was rated highly under this heading. As a talented musician, Lady Strathmore herself introduced them to the piano. Like her mother, Elizabeth was naturally gifted. She had a good ear and a sweet singing voice. Despite her small hands, she took immediately to the instrument. Piano practice was a pleasure (less so for David: it demanded all Lady Strathmore's firmness to keep him at the keyboard).

Later, both brother and sister were sent to the newly opened

Lady Strathmore supervised Elizabeth's education very closely

'Buffy' with her kitten. 'Some governesses are nice and some are NOT'

Pianoforte School in London, where they were taught by Madame Mathilde Verne and her sister. Madame Verne remembered Lady Elizabeth as a dear little girl, although her pupil was not always lovable. The strong streak of obstinacy that was to carry her through so many trials and tribulations in later life was already present. The preparations for a school concert prompted a typical display of wilfulness, recalled by Madame Verne:

> All the children had extra practice with an assistant teacher. One day, in what was called the Paderewski Room, I heard someone being taught an exercise that all the pupils detested.
>
> It seemed to me that the struggle was going on too long so I went into the torture chamber to find that little Elizabeth was the victim. 'We have only just begun,' said the teacher firmly. I looked at the child. There was a warning gleam in her eyes as she said to her teacher, 'Thank you very much. That was wonderful,' and promptly slid off the stool and shook hands to say goodbye.

Despite this rebellion, Lady Elizabeth learnt quickly and after six months took part in the parents' concert. 'She must have been a star performer because she played last, and it was always my custom to put the best player at the end of the programme,' said Madame Verne. Elizabeth's own recorded recollection of this occasion is somewhat painful: 'I got "out" in my piece and felt terribly ashamed.'

None the less, Elizabeth's relationship with her piano teacher was an enduring one. Their last lesson together was only six months before her engagement to the Duke of York. Then, not long after the wedding, Madame Verne was invited to tea: 'I remember that as I curtseyed the new duchess exclaimed, "You must give the Duke some lessons. I have already begun to teach him his notes and he knows three."'

Dancing was another skill required of a young girl before she could be launched into society. Lady Strathmore rejected the modish London dancing schools of the day and chose instead to employ the famous fiddler Mr Neil to teach 'her Benjamins' their steps. Although it is unlikely that Elizabeth remembered it at the time, Mr Neil had already played a central role in her earliest childhood memory. This was the occasion of the great family reunion at Glamis for her grandfather's golden wedding celebrations, when she had been barely three years old. Mr Neil and his String Quartet had been one of the main attractions at the festivities, where Elizabeth had watched the guests energetically dancing reels by the light of Lord Strathmore's Chinese lanterns.

Mr Neil (no one even then knew his first name) was a celebrated figure in Highland high society. He and his band seemed to appear at every kind of gathering. No visitor left a house-party, even at the grandest castle, without being charmed by his old-fashioned high spirits. By the time he was engaged to teach Lady Elizabeth and her brother he was already an elderly man, with more than half a century of fiddle-playing behind him. He presented a strange sight: his long white beard was quite worn away on the left side of his face where he pressed the instrument to his cheek. And he always wore stout brown walking boots, even on the most formal occasions.

Despite his unnerving appearance, Mr Neil was a kind-hearted man, skipping vigorously around the room after the children as he played. He taught them not only the fashionable dance steps of the day but also the mazurka and the minuet, which for a time became their party piece. David and his sister grew very fond of him.

As the Strathmore children capered to Mr Neil's tunes, the grown-up world had other preoccupations. At the end of April 1910, King Edward VII caught a severe cold. His condition worsened and the nation – especially that small aristocratic segment of it to which Elizabeth's family belonged – grew anxious. Daily bulletins were issued. Both the King's wife, Queen Alexandra, and the King's mistress, Alice Keppel, stood vigil at the royal beside. On 6 May, Edward died.

Three days later the accession of his son, King George V, was proclaimed from St James's Palace:

> Whereas it has pleased Almighty God to call to His Mercy our late Sovereign Lord King Edward the Seventh, of Blessed and Glorious Memory ... We, therefore, the Lords Spiritual and Temporal of this Realm ... with Numbers of other Principal Gentlemen of Quality ... do now hereby, with one Voice and Consent of Tongue and Heart, publish and proclaim That the High and Mighty Prince George Frederick Ernest Albert is now, by the Death of our late Sovereign of Happy Memory, become our only lawful rightful Liege Lord George the Fifth ... God Save the King!

The proclamation was marked with mass playings of the National Anthem, crowds swarming down the Mall and a royal gun salute in Hyde Park.

The coronation took place a year later on 22 June 1911 – an event that was to have a profound effect on the ten-year-old Lady Elizabeth Bowes Lyon who at that stage could not have dreamt that one day she would be crowned Queen herself. In an essay aptly entitled 'The Coronation', which still exists in the Glamis archives, she gave a breathless account of the occasion:

OVERLEAF: The coronation procession of George V and Queen Mary

51

At about half past ten in the morning I, Rose, Mother and Pat started for London and got there at about one o'clock. In the evening we went to a lodging in Westminster. At about six in the morning we got up and had our breakfast and started, and after a lot of trouble we got to the Aquarium.

When we had been in our seats for a little time, the Grenadiers marched up with their band and after a time the Grenadiers began to play. Then the sailors came up and got in a double line. At about twelve o'clock Lord Roberts and Kitchener arrived. About twelve, two hundred Indians rode along, and then the Lifeguards came along, and then King Edward [sic] came along. And then the Lifeguards went away and we went to have some refreshment and then we went to our seats.

At half past one the King came out of the Abbey and after saying a few words to some gentlemen drove away with Queen Alexandra [sic] and the Lifeguards followed him with Lord Roberts. And then the sailors marched away and then we went away and of course we had to walk!, May, self, Rosy and Annie.

Shortly after this, Elizabeth and David embarked on a marvellous foreign adventure. They were to pay a visit to their maternal grand-mother, Mrs Scott, in Italy.

After she was widowed for the second time in 1889, Mrs Scott divided her time between her English home, Forbes House, near Ham Common in London, and the Villa Capponi at Fiesole, high in the hills overlooking Florence. Her grandchildren were to travel to Fiesole, escorted by their spinster Aunt Violet.

In honour of this special holiday, summer clothes were ordered from Gorringe's department store; sunhats and straw bonnets from their favourite milliner's. Servants packed trunks and assembled them in the hall ready for departure. When the moment came to leave, Elizabeth and her brother were too full of anticipation to feel sad at leaving home. Besides the thrill of travelling to a foreign country, they were fond of their grandmother and were looking forward to seeing her again. They often stayed with Mrs Scott in England and, knowing her, had every reason to look forward to a wonderful holiday.

The journey to the coast was fun; the voyage across the Channel thrilling. But it was the sleeping compartment on the train that enraptured them. It had white linen sheets and a wash-basin that really worked. And then, there was the restaurant car: the rattling array of cutlery at their little table, the white-jacketed waiters and – for children brought up on plain and wholesome nursery meals – the chance to choose exactly what they wanted to eat from a lavish menu, all contributed to an intoxicating experience. Even with their aunt

54

Mrs Harry Scott, the
children's grandmother,
whom they visited in Italy.
The trip made an ineradicable
impression on Elizabeth

A final photograph with David
before he left for prep school

there to supervise them, they enjoyed being treated like grown-ups for the first time in their lives.

As the train sped south, they climbed happily into their bunks for the night. The long journeys to and from Scotland had accustomed them to the click of the rails and the swaying of the carriages. But the exotic sounds and smells of that night-time journey were new. So too were the place-names as the sleepy children opened half an eye whenever the squeal of brakes signalled their arrival at another brightly lit station.

Eventually they pulled in to Florence and their first encounter with foreigners *en masse*. Used to the reserved ways of the Scots, the children were amazed by the vociferousness and wild gesticulations of the Italians.

Leaving the chaos of Florence station, the party made the slow journey uphill to the Villa Capponi. Mrs Scott's house was set amongst magnificent cypress trees, which stood out sharply against a background of hazy blue hills. According to Lady Cynthia Asquith:

> Inside everything was in perfect harmony with the surroundings, and one can imagine how impressive to a child must have been the great room with an organ at one end, a fire-place in the centre and dark panelled walls – a stately solemn room, yet full of comfort and brightness. Lovely furniture, flowers, books, beauty everywhere. And the little chapel with its few exquisite pictures, and walls covered with red damask.

The sun shone and the children flourished. There were visits to the Pitti Palace, the Boboli Gardens, the *trecento* frescoes and, most memorable of all, the Medici tombs. Elizabeth took a keen interest in her grandmother's garden, helping with the weeding and planting out. Together they discussed new improvements, including the building of a little summer loggia. Long after the holiday, regular news bulletins about the progress of the garden arrived from Italy. In one letter, Mrs Scott asks her daughter to tell 'that sweet child Elizabeth that the Blood Orange tree is covered with fruit this year'.

The trip was one Elizabeth would always remember. Italy made an ineradicable impression on her. Seventy years later, she borrowed the Royal Yacht *Britannia* from her daughter especially to visit Venice. She had glimpsed La Serenissima from a train window as a child and had vowed that she would visit the city at least once in her lifetime.

Another glimpse of Elizabeth's life in those golden pre-war summers is to be found in the diaries of a regular visitor to Glamis, the Bertie Woosterish Freddie Dalrymple-Hamilton, who was to remain a life-long family friend. Already infatuated with Rose, here he records his first meeting with her younger sister in 1911:

August 15: Met Charles, a cousin, on his way to Glamis.

Arrived 5.30. My first visit. Very pleased to see Lady Rose again. Made the acquaintance of her younger sister Elizabeth for the first time who is a little angel!!!

August 16: Played tennis most of the morning. Cricket in the afternoon at Forfar. We made 200 for 8 after which the more energetic ones set out to climb a hill about three miles off. Elizabeth and I thought this quite beyond our strength and we hurled ourselves down and went to sleep on the top of the first hill. We got back about four or five o'clock and played tennis. After dinner we sang ribald songs in the billiard-room and later danced in the drawing room. I won my shilling off Rosie by sitting alone in the Hangmen's Room in the dark for five minutes at midnight !!!

August 19: Fancy dress – Elizabeth in an early Georgian kind of rig. We danced reels in the middle of which my bags fell off and I had to make a quick exit!!!

August 20: Chapel. Sat next to Michael and much ado not to laugh. Nearly everyone else went to see the Clintons but Rosie, Elizabeth, Rupert and I went for a trout tickling expedition and had great fun though the number of trout tickled was not exactly big! Fear we rather shocked some of the local parishioners who we met in the course of the afternoon. Also visited the wishing well and recorded a wish. Rosie proved her strength by carrying Rupert and even me!!! Elizabeth nearly killed herself eating green apples.

August 21: Railway strike over so had to leave. Very annoying as I don't think I've ever had such a good time as in the last few days. A large party including Elizabeth came to the station to see me off. I carefully left my watch behind but Elizabeth went back and just got it in time. The rotten train came alright and I left them all, wishing more than I can say that I hadn't got to but these things can't be helped. I had a mad desire to leap out of the carriage at the last minute ... Got to Edinburgh and sent Elizabeth her box of chocolates.

Staying with the Strathmores at their Hertfordshire home, St Paul's Walden Bury, the following year was just as much fun. Again Freddie's diary paints a boisterous picture:

April 12: Rather energetic in the evening playing tennis etc. Lady Rose and I being rather good at it! Played some weird game after!!!

April 14: Church – walked back through the woods and had a long rest under a spreading chestnut tree on the way. We were beautifully idle the rest of the day lying in various attitudes of repose on the lawn though one or two efforts were made to play tennis. Lady Rosalinda and I went for another walk after tea and slept under a tree for about an hour.

Had appalling struggle with Mike on the lawn afterwards and had most of my clothes torn off me! Later aching.

April 15: Mike, Lady Rosie, Elizabeth, David and I went down to The Grotto and had certain adventures with an old boat which Mike succeeded in sinking before we'd done with it.

July found Freddie back again. 'Played tennis etc. after tea and got very overheated. After dinner a great curling match on the billiard-table.' The following day, after tennis and cricket, 'we went on a garden-robbing expedition accompanied by Rosie and Elizabeth, who did most of the eating. I fell backwards into a gooseberry bush which was rather a painful business. A gorgeous day in every way.'

The autumn that followed that carefree summer was a sad one for Elizabeth: in September 1912 David, her close companion in so many escapades, was sent off to become a boarder at a prep school in Broadstairs. This was St Peter's Court, a high-minded establishment where the little boys supposedly benefited from a regime of bracing sea air and constant prayer. It was a feeder school for Eton, where all Elizabeth's older brothers had been educated, as had the King's two younger sons, Prince Henry and Prince George.

Her brother's exile was a terrible blow for Elizabeth. She was desolate. 'David went off to school for the first time on Friday,' she wrote to a friend. 'I miss him horribly.'

In a typically affectionate letter to her mother from Scotland she wrote, 'My Darling Very Precious Lovable Love: I hope you had a very good journey. Please give every kind of message to David. And do bring him up if you can. Lovie I was so sorry to have cried when you went away.'

A little later, when Lady Strathmore had taken David back to school after the holidays, Elizabeth wrote in similar vein: 'I hope you had a very good journey down and also David. I miss you both very [underlined three times] much ... I shall write to David. Please give him lots of kisses from me.'

David eventually settled down happily at school, but at first was terribly homesick. 'Everything is very strange here and I feel very lost,' he wrote to his mother. Elizabeth tried to comfort him, despatching letters and postcards almost daily to her 'darling bruver'.

Lady Strathmore felt for her daughter's loneliness and worried about her pale face and loss of weight. Swift action was clearly needed. Boarding school was discussed as a possible option. Several of Lady Strathmore's friends were also contemplating the idea for their daughters. But after much thought, she decided against taking such a drastic step and settled instead on the Misses Birtwistle's Academy at No. 30 Sloane Street, not far from the family's home in St James's Square. The bustle of school life, her mother hoped, would cheer her daughter up.

The Misses Birtwistle treated the education of girls with the utmost seriousness and offered their pupils a broad traditional curriculum. Elizabeth joined Class 3, where she was taught grammar, arithmetic, French, English composition, English literature, spelling, recitation, geography, history, scripture and natural history. It was a demanding workload for such a young girl, especially since she had to fit in piano and dancing lessons as well. Even so, according to surviving school reports she seems to have coped well, gaining high marks in all subjects except maths.

Elizabeth showed a particular flair for English. She was often awarded the maximum marks for a piece of work; and at the end of the school year her parents watched her carry off the literature prize

The weekly report from the Misses Birtwistle, which Elizabeth had to bring home to her mother every Friday afternoon. Would she have been top of the class had she not been 'absent' for Literature and Geometry?

for one of her essays. History, thanks to her early reading, was another subject in which she shone. So was scripture, which delighted the devout Lady Strathmore. Her French remained near perfect, a tribute to the efforts of Mademoiselle Lang and her successors. It was only in arithmetic that she had problems, in one test scoring seven out of twenty possible marks.

The Misses Birtwistle were kindly and intelligent and Elizabeth flourished under their benign regime. She enjoyed the company of her fellow pupils and giggled at silly jokes with the rest of them. She was popular with her teachers, too, never scoring less than thirty out of thirty for good conduct. Nevertheless after only two terms Lady Strathmore decided, somewhat perplexingly, to remove her daughter from the school. However successful the Birtwistle experiment had been, she probably felt, as did so many of her class and generation, that girls were still best brought up under the eyes of a protective mother and a sensible governess. As for Elizabeth, she seems to have been quite happy to comply with her mother's plans.

This was certainly not the end of her education. Another governess was engaged to school the children during the Easter holidays: Kathe Kubler, otherwise known as Miss Fräulein. 'It was really just chance that I taught Lady Elizabeth,' according to Fräulein Kubler. 'I was in London in a German governesses' hostel. One day Lady Strathmore asked for one of us for her children and I was suggested. She interviewed me – and that is how it happened.'

Miss Fräulein soon became firm friends with Elizabeth, but not so, unhappily, with David. For some reason he took a violent dislike to the German governess and spent his holidays cataloguing her faults. Although his sister pleaded her case, he was determined to oust her.

His opportunity came unexpectedly one day when he was taken shooting for the first time. He managed to bag a hare and returned triumphantly to Glamis bearing the corpse. Suitable praise was lavished on the great hunter and the kitchen was instructed to cook it for the schoolroom lunch. Unfortunately on the day of the lunch the children arrived home late having been delayed in Dundee, and when they sat down to eat they found nothing left but a pile of bones and the poor creature's head. The hearty Miss Fräulein, who was built on extremely generous lines with an appetite to match, had demolished the lot and was just wiping the last drops of gravy from her lips. Elizabeth tactfully kept silent but David was outraged and stormed off to complain vigorously to his mother.

Despite attempts to placate him, David refused to forgive. Lady Strathmore was faced with the inevitable. Miss Fräulein and her many cases departed from Glamis, leaving the staff with lasting memories of how she used to shake the castle to its very foundations with her Teutonic tread.

The date of this dramatic parting was 10 July 1914: the outbreak of the First World War was less than a month away. However, the story does not end there. The kind-hearted Elizabeth kept in touch with her old governess and the two of them continued to correspond throughout the war. As Elizabeth helped her sister Rose to nurse British soldiers at Glamis, which became a hospital for wounded servicemen, her stout friend on the other side of the Channel was caring for German casualties in France. Despite the fact that one of her brothers, Fergus, had been killed at Loos and three more were wounded at the front, Elizabeth remained true to Miss Fräulein.

For her part, surviving letters from Kathe show how fondly she felt about her former pupil. One is dated 27 September 1917 – part of a remarkable correspondence across enemy lines between a young British aristocrat and her former German governess. 'My darling Elizabeth,' it reads:

> Thank you so much for your letter which I loved to get. I am always so glad to hear of you and to hear all your news. How very, very sad that three of your brothers were wounded and Lord Glamis seems to have been pretty bad ... You are quite right! We had too nice times together to ever forget each other. How is Lady Strathmore and Lady Rose? I expect very busy with nursing and very good at it. How sad that you have not grown! Are you still lying down after lunch every day? You used to like it so much, didn't you?

Kathe goes on to enquire about their mutual friends at Glamis and continues, 'Has Juno had another baby this year, puppy you call it, don't you? You see I want to hear everything and you must write soon and answer all my questions. Will you, old Buffy?'

On another occasion Kathe wrote:

> No, I am not going to marry at all, though somebody asked me to some time ago, but I do not think this is the right time now at all for weddings and things, though my sister Ottilie thinks very differently and got married on August 1. I want to nurse and nothing else, as long as this dreadful war is lasting. Some time ago Thea and I were asked to go to the front as nurses and we simply loved to go. We were sent as far as Cambrai in France which is a German town now. We are both nursing here in a big Red Cross Hospital, which was a girls' college formerly and is now filled with wounded German soldiers. We have lots of them and are dreadfully busy as new patients are arriving by day and night. Hard fighting seems to be going on just now. We hear the cannons roar all day long from Arras.

The letter is signed, 'I am always your very loving old friend, Kathe.'

In another letter, which reached Elizabeth via the English consulate in the Hague, Kathe asks: 'I wonder is Lady Rose married by this time? And what are you doing? You have forgotten all your German, I am sure.' Touchingly she adds, 'I shall never forget you.'

Many years later, after the end of the Second World War, we hear of Kathe again. A cutting from the *Daily Express* dated 18 August 1946, speculates that the little market town of Erlangen, near Nuremberg, was never bombed by the Allies because it was the home of a schoolmistress called Kathe Kubler, and Fräulein Kubler had once been the governess of the Queen of England.

Kathe, who had never married, had suffered under the Nazis because of her part-Jewish ancestry. She had been removed from her post as headmistress of a girls' school at Naumburg, near Leipzig. Now reduced to living in a tiny attic room furnished only with bed, washstand and a shelf of schoolbooks, she had proudly shown off her most prized possessions: three letters from Lady Elizabeth, now Queen of England, a signed photograph of The Queen with the two princesses, and a collection of snapshots taken at Glamis thirty-three years earlier.

Kathe told the *Express* reporter that the greatest day of her life had been in 1937. A letter had arrived from Queen Elizabeth. It proposed that Kathe visit her old friends in Britain. No sooner had she set foot on English soil than she received an invitation to Buckingham Palace. At four o'clock that same afternoon she sat down to tea with The Queen. It was a magical reunion: 'Her Majesty was so friendly and so kind. Everything was so lovely; there were such wonderful little cakes. We just talked and talked.' Three hours later Kathe left carrying a huge bunch of carnations, a present to an old governess from a faithful pupil.

The Bowes Lyon governesses were were not always so popular. In an early essay entitled 'The Sea' Elizabeth got no further than a single damning line in her exercise book: 'Some governesses are nice and some are NOT.' Such strictures could never have applied to Miss Fräulein's immediate successor, the amiable Mademoiselle Madeleine Poignard. A charming note from her to Lady Elizabeth survives, obviously written late at night and slipped under the bedroom door. Although Elizabeth had now turned fourteen, she was perhaps not the easiest of pupils ...

'You asked me today if I should be able to write a whole composition in English; did you not!' wrote Mademoiselle Poignard. 'I shall prove to you how unclever I am when I must speak English, or more, write it.' She continued:

> I should be very pleased to know if you are really satisfied with your French lessons; do they not seem to you much too long and uninteresting, and are you not looking with much impatience your watch, that it gives you hope of being soon liberated from your disagreable teacher. I do hope no, but it is rather difficult to imagine what other people are thinking about you, especially when you are a foreigner. And now, what do you think of my English language? It is rather bad is it not? and don't you believe that I am right in still remaining one year in England to better it?

Elizabeth must have been trying to frighten poor Mademoiselle Poignard with ghost stories about Glamis, for her governess goes on bravely to say: 'I am awfully pleased to be here in Scotland, and in such a beautiful castle; but you could tell me how many stories and legends about it that it pleases you, I should not be afraid of being left quite alone for a whole night in it. Laugh at me if you mind, I don't take back my words!

Elizabeth composed a humorous account of how one of these terrible monsters was captured and destroyed. Entitled 'The Devilfaced Spider of Glamis' it was gruesomely illustrated:

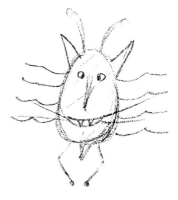

> It resides in the Red Room, where it was nightly hunted with great vigour by the Ladies, Lyon, Dausen Day and Glamis, with no result. In 1914 this frightful animal was valorously decimated by Arthur Barson Esq., after a long and exciting chase.
>
>   His only weapon was a preserving knife, and for this great deed of valour he was presented with the Iron Cross of the First Order. The remains were buried with great pomp in the flower garden, and now on stormy nights, when the wind howls drearily around the old castle, the stamps and curses of the Spider and Barson can be heard mingling with the blast.

As Mademoiselle Poignard quickly discovered, if you took on Lady Elizabeth you had to be prepared for a great deal of teasing. One day, to her alarm, she received a mysterious letter. Disconcertingly, the sender's address was Bedlam L.A., London, E. It was dated 2 December. 'Dear Madam,' she read:

> It is now 7 years since you left the Asylum, cured of your hallucinations. Your unfortunate attacks are due to return Dec. 29! We are keeping a bed for you in case you wish to return. Doctor Waring, the man you tried to murder with a carving knife is not quite recovered, and is awaiting your return with great eagerness. I think it would be advisable to return here on the 28th if possible, as we cannot vouch for your reason after that date. You should be out again by February at least.

Elizabeth Lyon
born the 4th day of August in the year 1900,
passed the OXFORD PRELIMINARY LOCAL EXAMINATION in the year 1914
at the London Centre,
under the Index Number 3.

The Candidate satisfied the Examiners in the following Seven Sections:—

Arithmetic
English History
English
Geography
French
German
Drawing

Elizabeth Lyon

Dictée

19 août 1914

Bonaparte. — Campagne d'Italie.
Ce fut une étonnante fortune que la sienne. Il était né en Corse au en 1769 au moment où cette île devint Française (1768). Simple lieutenant d'artillerie quand la Révolution éclata, il releva ses talents au siège de Toulon. En ce temps là on devenait vite général. On fut étonné cependant, lorsque le Directoire le nomma général en chef de l'armée de d'Italie. Il avait vingt-sept ans. Mais dès les premières batailles, son génie s'imposa à tous. Il fit des merveilles avec une armée 38,000 hommes, auxquels il promettait, non seulement la gloire, mais la richesse. C'est une promesse que les généraux de la Révolution ne songea pas à faire. En trois mois, il fut maître de toute l'Italie du Nord. Il bloqua la forte place de Mantoue. Quatre armées essayèrent en vain de lui faire lever le siège. Il les battit, en changeant sans cesse de procédés; il attendait

1.2.3. Villes au Nord de l'Italie.

The Duchess is still here. I don't expect you remember, but you tried to strangle her the same week you nearly murdered Dr Waring. Your attacks of madness will return every 7 years, and I am writing to warn you, as you were always one of my favourite patients. Hoping we shall soon be honoured by another and more prolonged visit.

I am your obedient servant,
John Beck M.D.

This ghoulish prank had been concocted by Lady Elizabeth and her friends Lady Lavinia Spencer and Lady Katharine Hamilton. It was very much in keeping with their taste for zany schoolgirl jokes, including riddles of the very silly variety. Some painful samples survive, carefully recorded on Glamis' headed vellum paper.

'Why,' they asked each other, 'are women like telegraphy? Because their intelligence is far in advance of the mail.' Or, 'What are the Poles doing in Russia? Holding up telegraph wires.' And, 'Why am I worth twice as much as you? Because I am double you, o man.' While this poser has an authentic ring of the times: 'When did the Kaiser count his chickens before they were hatched? When he heard Von Kluck!'

In the summer of 1914, Lady Elizabeth passed the Oxford Preliminary Local Examination in seven subjects: English, arithmetic, history, geography, French, German and drawing. Weeks later, war was declared and her formal education effectively came to an end. Europe was about to be convulsed by bloodshed. Glamis Castle would shortly become a military hospital. And Elizabeth would learn all too soon about coming to terms with pain and bereavement.

Elizabeth's school-leaving certificate. Note the simply 'Lyon' surname

French Dictée. Despite being teased by Elizabeth, Mademoiselle Poignard coached her charge to a high standard

CHAPTER FOUR

Elizabeth's war

· · · ❦ · · ·

IT WAS ON Elizabeth's fourteenth birthday that her future father-in-law, King George V, wrote in his diary: 'I held a Council at 10.45 to declare war with Germany, it is a terrible catastrophe but it is not our fault . . .'

The omens had been gathering all summer. In June the Archduke Franz Ferdinand, heir to the Austrian throne, had been assassinated in Sarajevo. Throughout July and August the rulers of Europe had been aligning themselves for war. Week by week, country by country, they took sides.

Despite the gravity of the news, the small, well-regulated world of families like the Bowes Lyons continued on its normal course. At Glamis, the castle's twenty-eight bedrooms were being prepared for the annual influx of summer guests with their guns, rods, servants and dogs. The 'glorious twelfth' of August was approaching but Lady Strathmore and her younger children stayed in London, at 20 St James's Square, planning Elizabeth's birthday treat. It was to be a visit to a variety show at the Coliseum, where Charles Hawtrey and Fedorova topped the bill. The performance ended, the curtain came down and the audience clapped. Wilder applause and more gripping drama were to mark the real climax of the evening. The performers had taken their final bow when the theatre manager walked on to the stage. Britain, he announced, was at war with Germany. The whole audience erupted in an explosion of patriotic fervour.

'It all seemed so terribly exciting,' Elizabeth later recalled. 'People throwing their hats in the air, shouting and cheering. The atmosphere was electric and everyone couldn't wait to get at the enemy.' At midnight, as she lay in bed at home in St James's Square, she could still hear the huge crowds as they made their way down the Mall to gather at the gates of Buckingham Palace.

A formal portrait, made when Elizabeth was fourteen or fifteen

66

OPPOSITE RIGHT:
Patrick, having already served
in the Scots Guards,
transferred to the Black Watch
on the outbreak of war

ABOVE LEFT: Jock in the
firing line – he is standing
directly below the parapet
from which Elizabeth and
David poured their
'boiling oil'

CENTRE LEFT: Fergus,
who was killed in 1915 at
the battle of Loos

BELOW LEFT: Michael in the
uniform of the Royal Scots

That unique curtain call at the Coliseum on the night of her fourteenth birthday was to mark the end of Elizabeth's childhood. The four years of war that lay ahead were to transform her from a carefree girl into a young woman of uncommon warmth and understanding. Within months of the outbreak of war, she was to encounter both the extremes of personal grief and anxiety, and also the tragedies of others, ordinary people who had, until then, been utterly outside her circle of experience.

For the present, the mood was one of exhilaration. Freddie Dalrymple-Hamilton, a close family friend and sub-lieutenant in the navy who was to fight with great valour at the battle of Jutland, noted in his diary that day: 'Popular opinion seems to think we shall be home before Christmas. I doubt it!'

His pessimism was not widely shared. Although there was no conscription then, Elizabeth's older brothers, like thousands of others, had no hesitation about where their duty lay. Patrick was already in the Scots Guards. Jock and Fergus were in the Black Watch and Michael volunteered for the Royal Scots. As yet there was no hint of what was to be one of the most striking features of the forthcoming war: the horrendous rate of fatalities among junior officers, three times that of the men they led. Within a year one of Elizabeth's brothers would be dead. Before the war ended the family would be in mourning for another.

For the moment Elizabeth had no sense of foreboding. She told Lady Cynthia Asquith about the excitement of those first few days of upheaval when the routine of the schoolroom collapsed completely. She remembered 'the bustle of hurried visits to the chemists for outfits of every sort of medicine and to gunsmiths to buy all the things that people thought they wanted for war and then found they didn't.'

Meanwhile, Glamis was being hastily converted into a hospital. Within a week Elizabeth had left London and was installed in the castle. For the first time in her life she was without the companionship of her elder sister: Rose was training to be a nurse at the London Hospital, Whitechapel.

Freddie, a great admirer of Rose, noted in his diary: 'Went and had tea with Rosie at No. 20. Had a long yarn with her and talked a lot of nonsense and eventually saw her off to join the London Hospital in Bow Road wherever that is.' A few days later he wrote: 'Rosie told us some of her first-hand experiences of the London Hospital. It didn't sound very nice and I hope she won't kill herself over it!'

In Scotland, Elizabeth was also at work. There was much to be done: the billiard-table was piled high with 'comforts' for the troops;

68

parcels had to be assembled and sent off; the soldiers needed thick shirts and socks, mufflers, bodybelts and sheepskin coats that had to be cut out and treated. She told Lady Cynthia: 'Lessons were neglected for during those first few months we were so busy knitting, knitting, knitting and making shirts for the local battalion – the 5th Black Watch. My chief occupation was crumbling up tissue paper until it was so soft that it no longer crackled, to put into the lining of sleeping bags.'

Freddie was one grateful recipient. 'Lady Strathmore gave me the most gorgeous sleeping bag which she had made for me and I think it will be my most valuable possession in the cold and wet days to come,' he wrote.

In December, the first wounded soldiers arrived from Dundee. They were comfortably installed in the oak-panelled dining-room, which had been turned into a ward. Rose, who had returned from her basic nurse's training, was in charge as Sister with Elizabeth as her willing assistant. Lady Strathmore made it plain that the men were to be treated as 'honoured guests'. Unlike other hospitals, there were no rules and regulations.

This was the first Christmas that Elizabeth had ever spent at Glamis. Traditionally, the family assembled at St Paul's Walden Bury. It was all the stranger because the gathering round the enormous tree in the castle's crypt did not include her brothers. However, the household enjoyed the festivities. One Gaelic-speaking guest recorded the lavishness of the crackers. 'After dinner,' he remembered, 'we all decided to pull them at once. There was a lot of joking and laughter. Something heavy and shiny fell into my lap. I picked it up and found it was a little Scottie dog made of solid gold. I later had it made into a brooch for my sister and my granddaughter has it still.'

The faithful Freddie arrived for New Year celebrations. On the last day of 1914 he wrote:

> It was awfully nice to see them once more and we had a most amusing afternoon. Rosie, Elizabeth and I went for a walk in a howling gale which nearly blew me away!
>
> Glamis is a hospital and there were 20 wounded soldiers there. We played tennis, doubtful card games etc. with them in the evening which was very amusing and after a bit, quite bawdy! It was a most CHEERFUL evening. Heard several new and wonderful trench stories and I can't say I envy the soldiers much!
>
> Pat, Jock and Mike are all at the front and Fergus is at Aldershot. I couldn't help thinking of the last time I was at Glamis with them all there and a cricket week going on etc. I never dreamt then the conditions under

which I should be there next!

We none of us sat up for the New Year for obvious reasons – anyhow very obvious on my part. I may not get many more nights in!'

On 1 January 1915, he wrote:

Blowing hard all day. Didn't stir out of the house till about one when Elizabeth and I ventured to walk about half a mile so as to raise an appetite for lunch. Rosie and I walked up to Gavin Ralston's house (factor) after lunch and back by the well. Nearly got blown away in the attempt.

Another evening with the soldiers but not such a long one as I went up to see David who's had 'flu and been in bed. He seemed full of life all the same. Rosie and Elizabeth arrived as well and we had long and rather dangerous, on David's part, talk about 'anatomy'!!! This because Rosie is joining the London Hospital and has been learning strange things out of a strange book!

Freddie Dalrymple-Hamilton as a sub-lieutenant in 1911. 'Got to Edinburgh and sent Elizabeth her box of chocolates'

The soldiers now became the focal point in the lives of Elizabeth and her mother. Everything was done to make them feel at home. One sergeant is quoted as saying: 'My three weeks at Glamis have been the happiest I ever struck. I love Lady Strathmore so much on account of her being so like my dear mother; and as for Lady Elizabeth, why, she and my fiancay are as alike as two peas.'

Those who were not bedridden ate their meals in the crypt, one of the oldest parts of the castle. Its stone walls were lined with ancient battle-axes, broadswords, suits of armour and wild animal skins. It became the scene of hideous stick-wielding rat-hunts. There were numerous kills.

In fine weather the soldiers explored the castle's extensive grounds or were taken on picnics in the surrounding hills. Indoors they took over the billiard-room, placed at their disposal despite its valuable tapestries. There were frequent singsongs, accompanied by Rose on the piano. They sang all the old and new favourites such as 'We Don't Want to Lose You,' 'The Sunshine of Your Smile' and 'Little Grey Home in the West'. Elizabeth's own party turn was her rendering of 'Strawberry Fair', which always guaranteed her a huge round of applause.

Freddie had by this time developed a fairly serious crush on Rosie. Her piano playing, not to mention her beauty, affected him deeply. 'R. played to us after dinner. She's wonderful on the piano and made me excessively serious. Sat and talked after some time,' he confided to his diary.

All day long, as the gramophone belted out George Robey singing

'Goodbye Dolly – I Must Leave You', the troops sat in the huge ward smoking and writing letters home. Sometimes Elizabeth helped with their composition. She caused panic on one occasion when she insisted on taking a photograph of Sergeant Ernest Pearne to send home to his mother. One of the sergeant's arms had been badly injured and his family had feared the worst. Unfortunately, such was the angle of Elizabeth's picture that the arm was invisible. His mother was distraught as she assumed it had been amputated. A second photograph, complete with arm in sling, was hastily taken and despatched.

Puzzles and games of patience were popular pastimes with the soldiers – as was flirting with their pretty nurses. One of Elizabeth's most frequent tasks seems to have been to run the mile up to the village to buy tobacco, cigarettes and sweets.

Lady Cynthia Asquith set the scene vividly:

> In the evening when it was cold and dark outside and the lights glowed in the ward, and great armfuls of logs blazed up the chimney, and the iron-studded door had creaked to and fro for the last time, and all of them were in; then the small tables were drawn up and rubbers of whist were played.
>
> It was at this time that Lady Elizabeth used to come down to play with the soldiers, and the nurses tell me how each one of them hoped she would sit at his table and share in his game, and how occasionally there were words because some aspirants thought others unfairly pushing.

Sergeant Pearne was obviously one of the favoured because he recalls that 'she was often my partner at whist and when she didn't know which card to play, she would tap her forehead with it and unwittingly expose its face. She got very cross when I teased her.' Other less charitable souls accused her of cheating.

One day for fun she raided the dressing-up box and kitted out her brother David, then aged twelve, as a fine lady in cloak, veil, furs and a sensational hat. She took him round the ward introducing him as her cousin. David asked all the polite questions such ladies would put to wounded soldiers and they complimented Elizabeth on her charming companion. It was not until later that they discovered the truth, although they had been suspicious of the pair's 'very merry mood'.

Sergeant Pearne had arrived in August 1915 with a shattered shoulder. He remembered his first encounter with 'the Imp':

> I first saw Lady Elizabeth shortly after my arrival, when I happened to wander into King Duncan's chamber (this was where the Scottish King

Lord Strathmore, Elizabeth, Lady Strathmore and Rose with an army sergeant in 1916

An unknown nurse and her soldier charges: the first wounded soldiers arrived from Dundee in December 1914

Elizabeth in nursing uniform … 'As for Lady Elizabeth, why, she and my fiancay are as alike as two peas'

Convalescing soldiers playing billiards – the site of 'ribald songs'

The autograph book, with a typical message from one of the soldier patients

A soldier's drawing in the autograph book. Another wrote: 'My three weeks at Glamis have been the happiest I ever struck'

Soldiers and nurses in fancy
dress. Elizabeth does not
appear – for once – to be
among them. Maybe she
took the photograph

died of his wounds after battle although Shakespeare has him murdered there by Macbeth).

There I suddenly came face to face with a huge brown bear, stuffed and standing on its hind legs with its mouth wide open. I got a rare fright and must have shown it, because the next thing I heard was someone roaring with laughter. Looking up I saw a cheeky little face at the window. Feeling a fool I glowered at her. It was only later I discovered who she was.

She was quick to see a joke and didn't she laugh when I and another lad, who also had his arm in a sling, tried to carry a large tray of plates, only to let them go crashing onto the floor.

The Strathmores gave concerts and dances for the soldiers. There were expeditions to the cinema in Forfar and the pantomime in Dundee. Lady Cynthia describes Christmases at Glamis as 'especially gay':

There were formal whist drives with much preparation beforehand, prizes set out for the winners, a bunch of flowers on each table, nurses super-latively starched, and the men aggressively clean with boots like looking-glasses.

When the prizes had been allocated, the soldiers would dance or blacken their faces, dress up in borrowed clothes – skirts and feathers – and to the music of numerous mouth-organs, march on the village, singing through the keen, windy darkness of the avenue.

If that did not alarm the locals, the arrival of a party of genuine Maori soldiers, on leave from the front, certainly did. The event is talked about to this day. Elizabeth showed them round the castle before drowning them in tea.

At night the soldiers were fond of telling ghost stories, no doubt inspired by Glamis's reputation for being bloodcurdlingly haunted. What Lady Cynthia does not mention are the serious poker games in which Elizabeth and her friends indulged. Numerous letters from troops once convalescent at the castle comment on her prowess at the table and enquire how she is faring with the Red Queen.

But life was not all fun and games. What stuck in the minds of a lot of the castle's inmates was the daily sight of Elizabeth anxiously waiting for the postman. 'She always rose early,' Sergeant Pearne recalled:

You would see this tiny dainty figure looking down the drive. She always stood in the same place. Every morning she was beside the cannon, with her black satin cocker spaniel Peter at her side. With so many friends and relations at the front, she wanted to be the first to know so she could look after her mother.

Her protectiveness was understandable. Apart from her great affinity with and love for her mother, she knew only too well what effect the arrival of one of the dreaded black-edged telegrams would have on her 'darlingest lovie'.

Lady Strathmore had already lost two of her ten children before the war began. Violet had died of diphtheria before Elizabeth was born and Alexander – Alec – had died of a brain tumour in 1911.

Sadly, Elizabeth's vigil paid off. One morning towards the end of September 1915, the dreaded telegram arrived. Fergus – the wag of the family – was dead, killed in the battle of Loos. Sergeant Robert Lindsay, who had been with him when he died, wrote a few days later to Lady Strathmore to tell her what had happened. He gave a graphic account, rather touchingly mentioning his own role in the third person:

> On the morning of 27th September, the 8th Black Watch were returning to the Brigade at about 4 a.m. and came to their own trench – very tired after two days and nights fighting around Loos.
>
> They were just preparing themselves some breakfast when Lyon came up to them with a paper in his hand and said: 'I am very sorry men but we have to go back again to the Hohenzollern to take some Germans out – it is a shame but we HAVE to go.'
>
> The men said the Captain had something strange in his eye as he read the message TWICE and seemed loath to go.
>
> They started off, some having swallowed some breakfast, but many without any. The Sergeant Major was drunk.
>
> As they were going up to the German trench, Captain Lyon leading, then came Sergeant Major Hill – then Sergeant Lindsay – all in single file. Then came the bombs – which fell at Captain Lyon's feet – shattering one of his legs – and he fell into Sergeant Hill's arms. At the same time he was hit by bullets in the chest and shoulder. Sergeant Hill and Lindsay sat beside him whilst he died and for two hours after and the last they saw of him was being carried away on a stretcher to be buried – but this is not certain.

Sergeant Lindsay not only sent Fergus's mother this letter but enclosed a black-edged envelope on which he had written in his copperplate handwriting, 'Bullet that was picked out of the left arm of the tunic of Captain the Hon. Fergus Lyon after he was killed in the Hohenzollern Redoubt on September 27, 1915, by Sergeant Robert Lindsay.'

Official sources were less truthful. 'I am very sorry,' they lied to the countess, 'to have to tell you that Fergus was killed in action on Sept. 27th at about 11.30 in the morning.'

78

The report continued:

A party of German bombers got into a trench we had captured from them the day before, and we were ordered to send a captain and fifty men to drive them out.

Fergus was the only Captain left and so took command of the party. He was leading his men up to the German trench when a bomb must have burst right on top of him, and blew his right leg off. Our doctor examined him, and told me that it was impossible for him to have suffered any pain as he must have died instantly from concussion.

The reporting officer, Cameron of Lochiel, also tried to spare the countess's feelings while explaining how military confusion had resulted in this tragedy: 'Fergus advanced to a trench we called "Little Willie", which we thought was clear of Germans and had been clear for some time. The Hun flung a bomb at your son which blew off his leg and killed him on the spot.' Perhaps in the hope of giving Lady Strathmore a little comfort, he added: 'The men who were with him at once charged and found thirty Hun in the trench whom they immediately bayoneted so he was promptly avenged by his own men.'

What gave a terrible poignancy to Fergus's death was that the family had only just seen him. A few days earlier he had slipped back to England for a 'few hours' of leave to visit his family and see his new daughter for the first time. He had married Lady Christian Dawson-Damer, daughter of the sixth Earl of Portarlington, only weeks before the outbreak of hostilities. This was their first brief reunion since he had left to fight. Ernest Pearne summed up the sense of shock: 'The Captain left on Monday night to return to his Battalion. The Battle of Loos began on Thursday and he was killed on Friday morning.'

Their little girl was called Rosemary Louisa. Lady Christian married again, but she had no more children.

The men billeted at Glamis recognised the depth of the family's grief. 'We agreed amongst ourselves,' wrote Sergeant Pearne:

not to go up to the billiard-room, not to play any games on the lawns, to keep piano and gramophone subdued, and ABOVE all, not to leave or enter the castle by the main entrance but by a side door.

We wrote our letter of sympathy and sent it to Her Ladyship. The next day a reply came back from Her Ladyship thanking us very much for our sympathy, and she and her husband hoped we would carry on EXACTLY the usual way and use the main entrance as before, as we were their guests. Those were SAD days.

Freddie Dalrymple-Hamilton went to stay at the castle in early November. Uniquely, the four pages of his diary for the time he was there were blank – save for the one word 'Glamis'.

Lady Strathmore spent much of the rest of the war trying to find out where Fergus had been buried. After extensive enquiries, a letter was eventually sent off on 25 October 1916. It read:

> The Countess of Strathmore is writing to Private William Vanbick – as she has seen Sergeant Lindsay a few days ago, who told her that Private Vanbick was the stretcher bearer, who buried her son Captain Fergus Bowes Lyon the 29th of September 1915. Lady Strathmore would be very grateful if Private Vanbick would kindly write to her and tell her about his burial – and if he can remember in what PART of the Quarry Captain Lyon was buried, Lady Strathmore would be very glad to hear – as she fully purposes to go out and try and find his grave when the war is over.

Sadly, Vanbick could not remember. There had been too many dead. But the search went on. Eventually, the countess's tenacity was rewarded.

A year after Fergus's death, disaster of a more domestic kind struck. It plunged Elizabeth, who had now turned sixteen, into yet another drama, though on this occasion one in which she had a central role.

The morning of 16 September 1916 dawned crisp and clear, perfect weather for shooting. Lord Strathmore pondered where the game might be at its finest on the large Glamis estate. David, the only male in the family too young to join up, favoured the eastern moors. Others disagreed. Finally the gamekeepers were summoned to resolve the argument.

The party of family and friends assembled outside the castle's main entrance, leaning on their shooting sticks and gossiping. Then keepers arrived with freshly oiled guns and spaniels barking at their heels. The beaters had their instructions and each man was handed a 'piece' – grouse sandwiches, biscuits and cheese, an apple and a bottle of beer. A wonderful day's sport was in prospect.

Lady Strathmore and Elizabeth waved them off before turning to face another busy day in the ward. Some twenty wounded soldiers awaited their attentions in the dining-room. Rose had married a young naval officer, William Spencer Leveson-Gower, during the summer and left Glamis, so now there was even more to do. The day followed the regular pattern. Beds were made, wounds dressed and letters written home. Elizabeth walked the mile into the village and back for sweets and tobacco. Those of the invalids who were able took a stroll in the grounds. As evening approached, the walking wounded set off for the cinema in Forfar, some eight miles away. Lady Strathmore and her daughter sat down to tea. It was five o'clock.

Meanwhile the earl and his party, anxious not to curtail an excellent day's shooting, were still out on the hill. The grouse had been plump and plentiful and there was enough remaining daylight to increase the bag. Coming over the hill, the earl looked down at the castle that had been his family's home for more than 500 years and thought he saw a wisp of smoke curling round the turreted roof. He drew his companions' attention to the sight, then pronounced that it was merely a smoking chimney.

Chimney fires were the bane of Lord Strathmore's life. The crypt had been turned into the soldiers' dining-room and they piled the logs so high in the huge fireplace that often old soot in the flue was set ablaze. The Queen Mother has recalled that one of their most vivid memories from those days was hearing the mad rush of soldiers as they dashed to the kitchens to get soup plates full of salt, then raced up the stone spiral staircase to the roof to pour their contents down a blazing chimney.

This time the family were not so lucky. Two soldiers, too ill to join their fellows on the cinema outing, thought they smelt smoke as they lay in the ward. They followed the scent through labyrinths of corridors and staircases until they reached a series of unfamiliar passages, dense with smoke, immediately under the roofs. They reached a dead-end and saw a door in front of them. The handle was hot to the touch and the paint was beginning to blister. As the door swung open, they were sent reeling backwards by a wall of flame. Hastily kicking the door shut, they hurried as fast as they could back down to raise the alarm.

The first person they came upon was Elizabeth. They told her there was a fire at the top of the Laigh Tower, the castle's ancient central keep, and that it already had a firm hold. Running down the stairs ahead of them she made for the telephone and, with great presence of mind, summoned not only the local fire brigade from Forfar, but the city brigade from Dundee as well.

The tower was nearly 100 feet high and there was a strong wind blowing. Already showers of sparks were raining down on the growing number of onlookers below. Great columns of flame could be seen curling through the roof, crackling ominously. To add to the hazards, the lead on the roof began to melt and streams of molten metal poured through gaping holes into the rooms below.

Minutes later the Forfar fire brigade arrived and began to unfurl the hoses. The thin jets of water from their manual pump made little impact on the blaze, which was now burning fiercely. At least there was no shortage of water. The River Dean flows through the castle grounds, running a mere 200 yards from the foot of the tower. Yet despite splicing several lengths of hose together, the firemen still could not get it to reach the riverbank.

As Elizabeth watched her home burn and waited anxiously for the Dundee brigade to arrive, a local drunk came shambling up and started to bother her with a mass of questions. How had the fires started? he demanded. Whose fault was it? Where were her father and brother? For once her manners failed her. Rounding on him, she exclaimed: 'You useless individual! Why can't you make yourself useful like everyone else? Can't you see I've no time for conversation?' According to reports of the incident, 'the lounger withdrew discomfited and ruefully enquired "Who's yon proud lassie?"'

In a desperate bid to save the castle, Elizabeth decided on drastic action. With the help of her mother and the household staff, she marshalled the large crowd of onlookers into long lines so that buckets of water from the river could be passed from hand to hand.

Another danger now threatened. The contents of an enormous water cistern at the top of the castle were poised to cascade on to the family's unique collection of paintings, tapestries and antique furniture. When the heat burst the great lead tank hundreds of gallons of water came flooding down the main staircase and into the principal rooms.

At that instant the shooting party returned. Armed with brooms and ignoring the fire raging above them, Elizabeth, her brother David and several friends stood in the doorways forcing the deluge further down the spiral stairs into stone corridors below. Teams were organised to remove the valuables, passing them along a willing chain of helpers, until all that could be salvaged was safely laid out on the lawn.

'Everyone worked with a will to remove what could be got at,' said a local report. 'The countess and Lady Elizabeth were especially energetic, the latter being "a perfect brick" as David Lyon remarked later when describing what she had done.'

'It was her little Ladyship told us how to do it and kept us to it,' one of his tenants told Lord Strathmore when thanked for his help.

Meanwhile the Dundee fire brigade had at last arrived and now sufficient water could be pumped from the river to begin controlling the spread of the fire. Even so, according to the *Dundee Courier* the firemen had considerable difficulty in getting at the fire because of the height of the buildings. 'In order to secure a good point of vantage several of them had to crawl over the roof, a somewhat exciting proceeding which was accomplished successfully.'

'Who's yon proud lassie?'
When fire raged through
Glamis in September 1916,
Elizabeth played a leading part
in fighting the flames

Surveying the damage:
Mr Ralston, factor, is on the
left; with Lady Strathmore,
David and Elizabeth. Most
harm was done by the
bursting of a roof reservoir.
Some of the damage can still
be seen today

Despite such daring, the firemen's efforts were initially to no avail. The blaze continued to spread as the frantic evacuation of the house continued.

The report goes on:

A huge column of smoke and flame rose high in the sky in the calm evening air and was seen for miles around. The towers and pinnacles, which are so characteristic a feature of the mansion, were blazing fiercely, but in the midst of the smoke and flame, the flagstaff remained intact, the Strathmore flag floating serenely above the mayhem.

For a considerable time the efforts of the brigades seemed to make little impression, but gradually the fire began to subside, and finally only the smouldering remains of the woodwork sent forth fitful gleams which were suppressed as soon as they appeared.

The cause of the fire was never established. Though mainly confined to the servants' rooms, the damage was spectacular. For weeks charabanc-loads of spectators came to view the blackened castle. One of the attractions, no doubt, was the knowledge of the part young Elizabeth had played in saving Glamis from being burnt to the ground. Her resourcefulness was toasted with 'Highland Honours' in every house and cottage for miles around. As the *Dundee Courier* put it, Elizabeth 'was a veritable heroine in the salvage work she performed even within the fire zone'.

From his trench in a far grimmer fire zone, her brother Michael wrote to his 'Darling Old Buffy' when news of the Glamis blaze eventually reached him. 'The fire must have been awful. I hear you worked like the devil himself.'

It is touching to imagine the young officer, enduring the hellishness of the winter of 1916 in northern France, thinking of his little sister's fight against the flames all those hundreds of miles away in his beloved Scotland. It was to be one of his last letters home from the front line.

The news when it came was as sudden as it was dreadful. Lady Strathmore and Elizabeth's elder sister Rose were in London. Telegrams from Glamis addressed to Rose were nothing unusual: they normally contained urgent but unremarkable instructions relating to the running of houses or the payment of bills. However, this time the message which was delivered to 20 St James's Square brought more heartache for the family.

That Lord Strathmore chose to address the telegram to his daughter indicates the effect he feared it would have on his wife. He wanted Rose to break the news gently to her mother and to be on hand to help her through this latest crisis. The telegram was dated 3

May 1917, and timed 10.45 a.m., Glamis. It said: 'Bad news. Michael missing April 28. War Office will wire further news. Tell mother they say not mean necessarily killed or wounded.'

Besides Fergus's death, the countess had already seen two of her sons badly wounded in the trenches. Now it seemed that Michael had also lost his life.

It was a terrible blow for Elizabeth, still in Scotland with her father, nursing the wounded at the castle. Michael, seven years her senior, was the brother who had always made a special fuss of her. As the youngest daughter in a large family of older brothers and sisters, she had looked to him as her mentor and protector. Her mother was fully aware of this and that same afternoon she wrote a note sharing her own grief with Elizabeth:

> So sad this terrible news of darling Mickie – Uncle Sidney has just been at the War Office and with great difficulty was allowed to see the casualty lists - and in the Royal Scots 16th Battalion 2 officers were wounded and NINE missing, so that is all we can hear for the present. He MAY be a prisoner with the 8th, or they may all be killed. Goodbye sweet darling. I wish you were here.

Uncle Sidney was not the only one to rally round. Everyone in the family used what friends and influence they had to attempt to find out what had happened to Michael.

A Private Riddle from A Company, 16th Royal Scots, was tracked down and interviewed. He reported: 'I am told and have every reason to believe it correct, that Captain Lyon was seen wounded, evidently in the leg or arms as he was lying on his back, pulling pins out of bombs by means of his teeth and then throwing them with his right hand.'

Lord Ellesmere wrote to Lady Strathmore's son-in-law Lord Elphinstone, Mary's husband: 'the only thing I heard was that Lyon was last seen having a devil of a fight - revolver in left hand firing for all he was worth: at the same time pulling out the pins (safety) of a bomb with his teeth and throwing with his right hand.'

Michael's commanding officer, Colonel Stephenson, tried to be comforting in his letter to Lord Strathmore:

> You will no doubt have heard by now from the War Office the sad news that your son Michael is missing! I would have written earlier but we have only come out of action today and I had no opportunity.
>
> Your son was leading his company against Roeux wood and village on the morning of the 28th of April. They got into the wood and village where they were heavily counter-attacked.

Battle of Arras, 1917, where Michael was captured

Some troops of the Brigade were captured by the enemy and it is quite possible that your son was amongst these - but I have not been able to get any definite news as to what Battalion the captured troops belong to.

I will let you know at the earliest possible moment when I get any further news. Waiting for news under these circumstances will I fear be an anxious time for you. I am deeply pained that I am not able to give any more satisfactory information but I sincerely hope that our next news may be that he is alive and well.

Lieutenant Oldric Portal's sister, a friend of Michael's, had a letter from her brother which she passed on to the Strathmores. 'Just a line to send you all my VERY best love,' he wrote to her:

We are up again now, as you know, and things are a bit sticky here just now. I've come up ahead to prepare the way for my company which comes up tonight. I will write as often as possible to let you know how we get on.

Such a terrible blow on arrival here. I was to have relieved Mike Lyon's

battalion and on asking for him found he is just reported missing. He was last seen going into a village from which none returned, as they were cut off in a show here three days ago that failed. It is a set-back that is going to be put right, and there is hope that he may be a prisoner, if not, perhaps I may find him soon. As you know I would love to, and perhaps he is somewhere out in front waiting for one.

I have a feeling he may be. I fear this makes my letter a sad one but I feel like Elizabeth. Only I am left. You know my feelings for Mike, I think we understood one another in a way most people do not.

I would write to his mother – but she may not yet have heard, so perhaps it is kinder not to. I don't know what to think of his Mother. She is so wonderful and brave, but this is just what one has always dreaded. Anyhow one must trust he is alright, as of course he must be, and perhaps I shall find him.

Lieutenant Portal wrote this letter on 30 April. Three days later he was killed in an unsuccessful attack on Roeux village – trying to rescue his friend.

Colonel Stephenson wrote to Lady Strathmore about the offensive in which Oldric died:

> We had all hoped that a second attack which we made would have brought us some news of all those who are missing, but unfortunately the Battalion that did the attack did not gain as much ground as was expected and they did not get to the point which Lyon and his company seem to have reached on the 28th and we could get no news from them.
>
> Some German prisoners that we took are reported to have definitely stated that a fairly large number of our troops were surrounded and captured in Roeux village, and it seems from other sources, that this was certainly the case. Unfortunately there is not the slightest clue as to who were taken and this will not be known until the lists arrive from Germany.
>
> Practically the whole of Lyon's company were cut off in Roeux when the enemy made a very big counter attack. His Company did splendidly in getting to their objective as they did and it is a tremendous grief to me that neither he nor any of his officers have returned and that such a large number of his men are missing.

With that brief note, the agonising wait for more news began. Jock, so badly wounded that he was then serving his country at the British Embassy in Washington, felt particularly helpless about his brother's plight. He wrote to his mother:

> I do hope I shall hear something soon as one feels so terribly far off. Darling Mother, it must be a perfectly dreadful time for you. One can only hope that you hear something definite soon. But please don't forget me because I want to hear EVERYTHING that you do.

A week later he wrote again: 'I see the Germans have taken quite a lot of our men prisoner, so there is always that hope. I wonder how long it takes to get the names through? Somehow I can't help thinking the dear boy will turn up all right.'

But hope was fading, Michael was now officially reported missing, presumed dead. David, the Strathmore's tenth child and Elizabeth's younger brother, was summoned home from Eton. The family went into mourning. However David, famous in the family for his uncanny powers of second sight, refused to believe that his brother had been killed. David Cecil, an old family friend, gave a graphic account of the fifteen-year-old's obstinacy:

> He lunched with me one day, and I pointed out to him that he should not wear coloured clothes and a coloured tie so soon after his brother's death.
>
> 'Michael is not dead,' protested David. 'I have seen him twice. He is in a big house surrounded by fir trees. He is not dead, but I think he is very ill, because his head is tied up in a cloth.'
>
> I pointed out that the War Office had reported Michael as killed and

they were not likely to have made a mistake, but David would not budge. 'Michael is not dead,' he maintained, 'because I have seen him twice, and I won't wear mourning for him.'

Some time later a bank statement for Captain The Hon. Michael Lyon arrived at St James's Square. No one had the heart to open it.

Eventually, however, someone had a look. At first glance the contents could only deepen the family's misery: a record of routine past transactions. And then one line of figures leapt out. Michael had cashed a cheque dated 4 May 1917. He was alive: 'Michael Lyon taken prisoner at Roeux 28th April. No news received of him until 18th May,' recorded the diary of the faithful Freddie Dalrymple-Hamilton. A friend of Michael's older sister Mary wrote her a note: 'You ought to get hold of that joyful cheque and get it framed.'

Then came Michael's own postcard, dated 4 May. It had taken three weeks to make the journey from Karlsruhe. Given his wounds, its sturdy tone was a testament to his sang-froid and strength of character. Nonchalant and practical, he wrote in a beautiful clear hand:

A postcard to let you know my address which is under my name. You can send me various things, chiefly food but I want an Auto-strop razor and lots of blades most of all. Did you get a letter from me? Got here last night after a long journey. I've arrived here with absolutely nothing except what I stand up in, but am getting a cheque cashed today. Nothing much to tell you on here I'm afraid but I hope I shall be able to write a letter shortly. Just going to have a bath. I'm perfectly filthy and a long beard. Love to all. Ideal milk, butter and bread and tea would be good, also shirts, vests, drawers, socks, flannel trousers (grey). Mike.

Bureaucracy took a little longer to spread the glad tidings. It was not until seven months later, on 7 November, that the family received official confirmation of what they already knew.

A Monsieur Emile de Torres, Secretaire particulier, wrote from the Belgian Royal Palace:

By order of His Majesty the King I have the honour of informing you, that His Majesty's Ambassador in Berlin has been able – through kind offices of Great Britain's representative here - to ascertain that Captain the Honble. Michael Lyon, of the Royal Scots, has been carried over on the 19th May, 1917 from Karlsruhe to the officer camp Strochen. He declares to be in a good state of health.

If the Kriegsgefangenensendung, or prisoner of war camp, was grim, Captain Michael Lyon never seemed to let it get him down. Elizabeth was his most frequent and devoted correspondent and his replies are full of life and fun.

After begging for more cigarettes in his parcels, 'still too far and few between', he went on:

> Lovely weather here lately and I have been playing miniature Baseball taught us by the Americans or rather Canadians. It's really quite an amusing game, but the most important part of it is the booing and cheering.
>
> The man who has the longest string of epithets and adjectives to hurl at his opponents is very good, and the great thing is to jeer and laugh at them till they get angry and put off their game. I am learning American slang for that purpose now.

In another letter, he wrote to Darling Buffy that:

> a most extraordinary happened the other day. We were in billets and one of my brother officers was returning after dinner and looked at the moon.
>
> There did not happen to be one that night and he saw the Union Jack. A few minutes later, he looked at a star. It was a dark cloudy night and no stars, and he saw the Honolulu flag mixed up with a poached egg.
>
> He is awaiting a Court Martial for drunkenness. But how marvellous! What can it all mean? Will Honolulu join in the war disguised as 'un vent en cocote.' Hurrah! 'Vive les Ouvriers! They'll make the Germans 'oller, moy word just 'ear 'em a 'ollerin, Ha. Ha. Ha. I guess he upset his thinking track some.

On another occasion he told her: 'the old gramophone is going most awfully well and we have played it all day, only though we are beginning to know the tunes rather well.'

So, as though it were the most natural thing in the world, POW Michael Lyon asked his sister to send fresh supplies: 'Mind you get me all sorts of nice records. One I want is "As She Goes Down Piccadilly" on one side and on the other "'Twas in November that I Remembers", both from Mr Manhattan.'

In July 1918 he wrote to his mother:

> The new exchange looks as though it might be quite good, though nothing official has been heard yet, but it would be very good if the 18 months is reduced to 14 and we get back to England in the end; I suppose the war may possibly come to an end before many more years.

Michael was referring to an exchange of hostages. To save money, prisoners of war were swapped on a regular basis through Holland. What the Strathmore family did not know, and the earl discovered only years later, was that Michael had given up his place for a transfer home in favour of a brother officer who was more badly wounded than himself.

His longing to be back in Scotland was obvious. He wrote to his

90

mother: 'In a fortnight or so people will be banging away at the old grouse again, and a whole shooting season wasted again, it's really rather wicked isn't it?' He also made an intriguing reference to Elizabeth: 'How is Buffy's heart?' he enquired mysteriously. 'I hope quite right again and that she is up to anything again.'

The war came to an end sooner than Michael expected. A week before the Armistice, the Strathmores had another piece of news, though it was inevitably tinged with sadness. Lady Strathmore's son-in-law Lord Elphinstone, Mary's husband, had a letter from his friend Dundas:

> By chance yesterday I came upon the grave of your brother-in-law, Fergus Lyon. Happening to pass that way, I was having a look at one of the most interesting parts of the old line, opposite Hohenzollern Redoubt. I was in 'The Quarry' which was a very well known spot in our system, just beside 'The Craters' near Vermelles.
>
> The quarry used to have a large number of officers' graves in it, but these have all more or less been wiped out, except Lyon's, which is curiously conspicuous through being absolutely intact. Several scores of others must have disappeared altogether, as the whole face of the earth about there has been blown up again and again. I suppose there is no place where fiercer fighting took place continuously for four solid years.
>
> It occurred to me that your wife or some of her people may like to know that the grave is by a very remarkable chance absolutely intact.

On New Year's Eve 1918 another telegram arrived. It was from Michael: 'Arrived here last night. Very nice too.' He was back in Blighty. Elizabeth and her family only just had time to rush to the station to meet the train.

CHAPTER FIVE

The Mad Hatters

· · · ⟨◈⟩ · · ·

THE MAIN TOWER at Glamis is one of the oldest sections of the castle. At the top of this great turret, up the 143 stone steps of its spiral staircase and by-passing the entrance to a secret passage, is a small room with a panoramic view over the park. It is immediately beneath the battlements from which the young Elizabeth and David poured water on their parents' unsuspecting guests. The room is lined with shelves, each one crammed with dusty box files and every box file crammed with dusty papers.

These are the castle archives. Not even the present Lord Strathmore knows exactly what they contain, although the work of cataloguing them is slowly progressing. Here are documents going back 500 years: game-books, account books, visitors' books, school reports, shoe-boxes full of photographs and postcards. Among this vast and varied collection are scores of letters which, were she to see them now, would take The Queen Mother back to her teenage years. Many of them are from her closest friends, the set of high-spirited society girls who called themselves the Mad Hatters.

Young women of Elizabeth's generation grew up more abruptly than their elder sisters had done. The war had a maturing effect on even the most pampered and protected of them, for few did not have a brother or a cousin at the front. Elizabeth, as we have seen, exchanged her schoolroom for a hospital ward, yet she and her friends enjoyed life to the full despite, or perhaps even because of, their wartime cares.

Two of the chief Mad Hatters were Lady Lavinia Spencer and Lady Katharine Hamilton, the co-authors of those dreadful riddles about the Kaiser and Von Kluck. Lady Lavinia grew up at Althorp and would be a great aunt of Diana, Princess of Wales, if she were still

In the garden at Glamis shortly after the war, with another favourite spaniel. James took the photograph, which he kept beside his bed

alive. Five foot five, slim, with big blue eyes and very good legs, Lavinia was full of spirit and not afraid to express her strongly held views with great candour. She loved reading, particularly the classics and Kipling. She played the violin beautifully and coolly practised on her Stradivarius as the Zeppelins raided London.

Lady Katharine Hamilton, the daughter of the Duke of Abercorn, was Elizabeth's other close confidante. Like Lavinia, she had known Elizabeth since early childhood and the three remained friends throughout their lives. In contrast to Lavinia, however, Katharine was shy and sensitive. Lady Mary Clayton remembers her well: 'She was very humble-minded, deeply religious and had a great gentleness about her.' However, for all her reserve, Katharine could be very lively. 'She had a marvellous sense of humour and when she got cracking, she was tremendous fun,' remembers her stepson, Major Raymond Seymour.

Another of the Mad Hatters was Betty Cator, who was to marry Elizabeth's brother Michael and go on to become Lady Strathmore. Her daughter-in-law, the present Dowager Countess of Strathmore, remembers her as 'tall, big and very jolly'. Like Lavinia, she loved hunting and was full of high spirits, perhaps a little too much so for her husband. When Betty became too excitable, Michael could be seen hiding under a bridge on the estate enjoying a cigarette until the storm had passed.

The innermost thoughts of this lively set are vividly recorded in their letters. The main correspondent is Lady Lavinia, whose zany sense of humour clearly appealed to Elizabeth. She showed a healthy streak of subversion, frequently writing under the pen name George R and addressing Elizabeth as Queen Mary. A typical piece of Lavinia nonsense reads: 'I always thought, me dear Mary, that you were a dreadful flirt, but now my suspicions are confirmed. For shame! Tut! Remember your queenly dignity, and don't make eyes at men in The Service, Mary – although, of course, I own it's a temptation. (Ssch).'

When they both confessed to being overdrawn at the bank and Elizabeth was concerned, Lavinia proposed a bold course of action:

Are you putting 'suitable for cinema acting' on your registration paper? I think we both act marvellously. The salary is big and the work light and amusing. You as the heroine who always believes in Him (sounds as though I was being pious!) altho' He is a black sheep and a dog, and me as the little widow. Shall us? Let's.

I am sorry you are feeling depressed. Don't, Elizabeth darling – I sympathise and know how some people make one feel a fat, hideous, stupid young fool – it makes one feel life is useless for weeks and then somebody nice comes along and one feels happy and not wanting to commit suicide any more. Do come south soon you saucy sly thing. Till death . . . Lavinia.

Saucy? Sly? Surprising words to see applied to Elizabeth. Her own family was conservative in outlook and behaviour. She and her mother prayed together every morning in the private chapel. Most of the earl's and countess's friends were strait-laced and traditional: the American diarist and socialite Chips Channon was the raciest among them, and the conduct of their eldest son's wife, with her cocktails and cigarettes, was positively beyond the pale. But J. B. Priestley was not alone in thinking that 'life on this high social level was strongly charged with sexuality' and these adolescent girls were certainly not immune to sexual attraction.

Both Elizabeth and Lavinia were enjoying crushes on the theatrical idols of the time – Lavinia's favourite was Basil Hallam while Elizabeth preferred another actor, Henry Ainley. There was also a good deal of teasing about Elizabeth's friend Freddie Dalrymple-Hamilton. Despite his being ten years older than Elizabeth and known to be in love with Rosie, Lavinia was constantly asking after him. 'How is your young man, Mr Freddie?' she enquired in one letter. And later, 'Are you enamoured of someone, barring Freddie?' Or have you jilted him?' In fact, Freddie was about to be jilted, not by Elizabeth but by Rosie. When he heard that Rosie had become engaged to a fellow naval officer, 'Wisp' Leveson-Gower, Freddie confided stoically to his diary, 'It didn't surprise me very much,' then added, 'Saw Charlie Chaplin for the first time. I must say he is extraordinarily funny and, in spite of everything, made me laugh very heartily.'

Freddie was not the only naval officer in the girls' thoughts. Lavinia again:

Katie is in town. We see a fair amount of each other. We were in church together today and a beautiful tall, fair Lieutenant walked in. How's F . . . ? Katie is settled to marry a sailor, but although I adore them, I think I should never bear my husband to go away for sometimes years at a stretch.

We have been to no plays at all this term. The result is that I am hungering after a divine face (of the opposite sex, of course!) and I believe we are going to *The Scarlet Pimpernel* with Katie – I would much rather go to a play I don't know much about with a young, heavenly actor in it. Is it true Basil has had an operation? Write and tell me all about Mr Freddie. Is it Dalrymple Hamilton or vice versa? I am aching for a real sentimental 'chat'.

ABOVE LEFT: Lady Katharine Hamilton and ABOVE RIGHT: Lady Lavinia Spencer – great aunt of Diana, Princess of Wales. Lady Elizabeth's two closest confidantes and co-authors of the dreadful riddles about the Kaiser and Von Kluck

RIGHT: Betty Cator, 'tall, big and very jolly'. She married Michael and later became Lady Strathmore

OPPOSITE: Letter from Lavinia (George) to Elizabeth (Mary). Lavinia's Goon-like sense of humour clearly appealed to 'Buffy'. The letter was written on both sides of folded paper, so pp. 1 and 4 are reproduced above and pp. 2 and 3 below

husky bass voice instead
of marriage and Mary!!
I crave your pardon, I am
blaspheming.

Freddy

Title of picture
Cuddling
Elizabeth

Tut Tut.
Write Soon
Yours George

PS My bruises are better but my ___ is still some sore.

Althorp.
Northampton.

Sunday

Dearest old Mary,
I am so so happy.
Guess why! Sub-Lieut Cecil
is at Spencer House &
is coming here this evening.
O, my yellow bags, green
whiskers and dirty teeth
what joy — He has got
four days leave — till Thursday.
Pip, pip my precious popinjay
poppet —
I damn, leave, dash
ly, blow, the, hang, 8.25 am bother

---

train, (b — y)(shhh) tomorrow
morning for London —
Ar'ent I a of sweet nature?
Many thanks for your two
letters — It is libel to say
I am a slacker, on the
contrary I am a hard.
-working woman — Hi ho.
You are a dreadful flirt.
Did HE (pshaw) cuddle you
in the train? I guess yes.

Elizabeth Hamilton.

Not so dusty; better that
than Elizabeth Ainley.
I nearly broke a blood
vessel in Church today, in
trying to keep solemn. We
had a Welsh priest and
his accent was extraordinary
and he never finished his
words —
chap = chapter, and what
was the worst was that
re continually said
Mare, just like we do in a

The Mad Hatters in costume.
Katharine Hamilton,
Mida Scott, Elizabeth and
Doris Gordon-Lennox

A later letter demands:

> Write at once all about the sailors – by return of post. Katie and I are dying for nautical 'juice'. She is still in Erin and a long way from the ocean blue, like your humble servant, George R.
>
> Forty wounded soldiers came to tea last week – I have had a letter from one since – aged 18 and 1 week. I am not allowed to keep up a correspondence with him but am going to send him cakes etc. when he returns to the war. O for a breath, a fleeting glimpse, a tender whiff of a boy in blue.

Katie Hamilton was equally fixated:

> Ever so many thanks for your letter. Yes, I had a most 'newsy' (!!!!) letter from Lavinia last week. Not a vestige of anything Blue about, D ... d luck, but I am going to an entertainment 60 miles away tomorrow and there may be one there.
>
> Just after I had written that I looked out into the garden, and lo and behold who should I see by the fountain. We saw him afterwards and I have just heard all about him from the gardener! He hails from New Zealand ... Wouldn't it be splendid if you and Lavinia and I all married sailors? There would be a lifelong feud between us if by any chance one of the 3 got promoted first!
>
> The post boy here drinks like hell and the other day he was steamed and the post was floating down a stream! Such is life. I hope your little friend F.D.H. has written you some nice 'juicy' epistles lately. Don't you always rush for the post? I do.
>
> ... Desmond says that he will never give me up till I give him up! What a liar! I know for certain that he is engaged to three young damsels (the 'ring' stage too).

Desmond appears to have been another young naval officer. In a later letter Lady Katharine announced, with the same proliferation of exclamation marks, that Desmond was to be sent to China 'for nearly two years': 'I feel so low about it especially as I know he can't come back without being engaged to some beauteous damsel or, if worst comes to worst, even a barmaid! You know what sailors are. I'd give my back teeth for a glimpse of something blue, something in Blue and Gold which smells of salt water and seaweed!'

Inevitably, the war intruded on the Mad Hatters' exuberance from time to time. In a letter of condolence after Fergus Bowes Lyon was killed in the battle of Loos in 1915, Lavinia wrote to Elizabeth: 'Thank you very much for telling me about your brother. It must be splendid to die like that.'

She went on to recount her own experiences in London:

The Zepps came last Wednesday but much to my surprise, I did not see them. It was about 9.30 and I was just in bed, but of course not asleep, when I heard the gun on top of Lloyd's Bank in St James's Street go off several times. It made little noise. The one in Green Park went off three times and the whole house shook like a jelly, including my bed!

I leapt up and to my amazement, Tom, our odd-job boy, rushed into my room, where Margaret [her younger sister] and I were sleeping. (I hope he liked my appearance in my nightgown and two plaits) ...

I got Margaret up and we dashed downstairs. (Quite a useless proceeding.) Downstairs the noise was inaudible, because it was all over. So I practised the violin for 20 minutes.

The war was not the only subject to depress a Mad Hatter. 'Cheer up old girl,' Lavinia wrote to Elizabeth on one occasion when she was feeling miserable. 'It is easier said than done, but you must not get melancholia at your tender age ... I nearly wept when I read about you having a plait. Well, I'm damned. Undo it at once; I am sure you look awful!'

As Lavinia well knew, Elizabeth was incapable of looking awful; in fact she was already famously attractive. Lord David Cecil, the Strathmores' neighbour in Hertfordshire had noted it when she was still a child. 'She had sweetness and a sense of fun,' he wrote, 'and a certain roguish quality.' Lady Longford's biography of Elizabeth stated that 'all the men were at her feet'. One of these was Lord Gorell, whose feelings embraced not merely herself but her whole environment: 'I was madly in love with her. Everything at Glamis was beautiful, perfect. Being there was like being in a Van Dyck picture ... the magic gripped us all. I fell *madly* in love. They all did.' Perhaps Lavinia was even slightly jealous when she wrote to her friend, 'Have you been behaving yourself well, lately? Please tell me the truth – Do you have dozens of male visitors to see you every day?'

Naturally, she would not have been allowed to see such visitors alone. Even at dances, well-connected young women like Elizabeth were never permitted to stray beyond the gaze of chaperoning elders. Occasionally, however, a breach of etiquette occurred, as an intriguing letter from a young man called Louis Hamilton shows. Like so much of the correspondence in the Glamis archive, it has no date, only the day, Thursday:

> I have been meaning to write to you for some days as I feel I owe you an apology – Bridget [wife of Dit Ogilvy, heir of the Earl of Airlie] tells me that you had it put across you for being absent so long (a mere 10 minutes I should say) at the Ball. I suppose being a mere male it was all my fault ... By the way I have still got a handkerchief belonging to you, which shall be washed ready for you to claim on arrival at Dartmouth.

Bruce Ogilvy, another of Elizabeth's admirers, had also noted her disappearance and felt compelled to write to her. 'I hear you enjoyed yourself very much at the dance!!! He is a capital young man ... do write to me and tell me all about how you are misbehaving your-self ... ' Today it is impossible to know how many raised eyebrows Elizabeth's brief vanishing act actually caused.

A letter from a sailor aboard HMS *Calistoga*, at sea off Yarmouth, might well have aroused even more disapproval, had it been seen by anyone other than its recipient. 'I hope you will forgive me for chucking you in this bald manner,' it says, and then proceeds mysteriously:

> I'm not going to beat about the bush with you, but I'm not going to come up to London anyhow this week (Betty tells me you know) as Marion Cook is in London and going about, and I think it best that we should not meet, under the circumstances. I do hope you will understand. Forgive me as but for this, I should have loved nothing more. Elizabeth, will you keep this to yourself?

One longs to know more. However, there were other admirers only too willing to step into his shoes. One of them, writing from Stanley in Perthshire, signed himself 'David J.C.G.':

> Since one is expected to write a thanking letter for a boring weekend, I do not see why I should not be allowed to write a genuine letter of thanks for a most delightful day. I enjoyed everything, the strawberries before lunch, lunch, even though your butler refused to give me potatoes and peas in his haste to bring you cold roast duck, *The Beggar's Opera*, the picnic with the exciting motor drives ...

Above all J.C.G. seemed to have liked 'playing gymnasts', even though these energetic activities prevented him performing on the piano after dinner.

Katie Hamilton was also having emotional problems. She had fallen for Lavinia's brother Cecil and wrote to Elizabeth of the romantic trials of unrequited love, although the jaunty last line indicates that her heart was not entirely broken:

> Last Saturday night I dreamt of brown eyes – with a twitch and long, soft, wavy eyelashes! You know the ones I mean. I am feeling a bit sore inside as I have had no news of Cecil – or rather about Cecil – for over 3 weeks. Bless his heart! It takes the biscuit to only see a man 3 times and fall in love with him so desperately that he remains supreme for nearly a year!!!! If I could but see him. Brief life is here our portion!
>
> Do you like the Marines?

If such affairs of the heart were primarily a product of their fevered imaginations, their passion for the London stage was real enough. Elizabeth had been an enthusiastic theatre-goer since childhood when she and her brother David drove through the darkened, frosty streets of London to pantomimes at Drury Lane.

As the children grew older so their tastes became more catholic. 'During the holidays, my sister and I used to go to theatres as often as we were allowed – usually in the cheaper seats, as our purses never bulged. She had a wide taste in plays, but I think Barrie's were her favourites, though Shakespeare was by no means slighted,' David wrote.

Drama was then enjoying a heyday, dominated by playwrights like George Bernard Shaw and Somerset Maugham who were highly respected as well as popular. Actors such as Basil Hallam, Charles Hawtrey and Gerald du Maurier were drawing huge crowds to the West End and the Mad Hatters wrote to each other rapturously about the shows they had seen, swapping notes about their favourite leading men.

Lavinia enthused:

A confession – look here, I am going to give up being cracked and silly about dear old Basil [Hallam]. It *is* silly, especially for me, as I don't suppose I shall ever hear or see him again. Of course it's a wee little more reasonable for you, as Ainley is still acting – I don't mean to be fickle and inconstant, for I still think Basil is a delightful actor, full of charm and altogether splendid but I am going to like sailors – it's such uphill work to go on adoring Basil – you'll think I am brutal, horrid, damned silly etc. I can't help it – I will tell you why perhaps some day.

Elizabeth's response must have been swift, for Lavinia wrote two days later:

My own – at last! Everything comes to he (or she) who waits. My dear you mistook my letter about Basil – I still admire him *frightfully* and think he is very, very beautiful and charming – but, to tell you the truth (for goodness' sake tear and burn this up) I have given up the thought of marrying him – don't laugh – I am very serious. I thought I was in love with him etc. and I may have been, but it's silly. It's age, my Mary, you know !

Don't say Mr Hallam is not worthy of me, he is – much too worthy – Don't tease me about it, will you ? I do like him just as much as ever, only I have just stopped being sentimental. Perhaps some day I will tell you why – I am awfully glad you still admire Henry [Ainley]. He is one, if quite, the best actor of the day. I do like G. du Maurier, do you? Of course, Basil is not such a good actor but he is so surrounded by charm ...

Don't you adore sailors?

102

Lavinia must have had second thoughts, for a little later she wrote, 'I have been rather unhappy lately about nothing at all – I expect the real reason is that I have had no "hero" for the moment! I always feel miserable when I have no special person to admire, don't you? But you always have such elegant and swellish sort of loves.'

The 'swellish' Henry Ainley eventually repaid Elizabeth's devotion, having perhaps noted the 'Lady' in front of her name. Not only did he send her a signed photograph, but also this letter, dated 19 March 1916:

> Ever since our first night in December last, which you were unfortunately prevented from attending, I have been meaning to write and offer you tickets for some other performance but I find I am not to have that pleasure, for I heard yesterday ... that you have booked seats for Friday evening.
>
> This being the case I can only express the hope that the play may come up to your expectations. I shall myself look forward with keen pleasure to Friday evening and at the end of the first act I shall raise my eyes to that part of the house where you and your friend will be seated, and may I hope to meet a smile of appreciation and pleasure.

He concluded in the same ingratiating vein: 'Having ventured so far, may I touch on just one other point, which is necessarily a somewhat delicate one – please remember that whatever my feelings may appear to be towards other members of the cast, they are purely and simply the attitude of an actor and not my real self.'

Lavinia may have been quite put out that Elizabeth had secured such a trophy. But she soon cheered up. Despite being confined to bed following a hunting accident, she had good news: 'A great uncle of mine died last week and left me £5,000! I shall no more be espoused for my beauty but for my money. Yum, Yum. I am an heiress ... I am much better but still keep to my bed – my bruises are rainbow coloured.'

Despite all the barely repressed ardour and adolescent sexuality inherent in the girls' letters, as far as unmarried young women of that era were concerned the rules of conduct were seldom breached. When they were, or looked as though they might have been, there was trouble. One of the Mad Hatters, Diamond Hardinge, risked disgrace when she and Rachel Cavendish went for a post-dance boating expedition on the Thames with some young men, led by Elizabeth's friend Bobby Somerset. Bobby was a sailor who later became a famous yachtsman. On this occasion, however, their rowing boat nearly sank, they had to be towed to safety by the river police and only the intervention of a royal equerry saved them from public scandal. A few short years later, Diamond tragically caught tuberculosis and died while still in her early twenties. Elizabeth was one of her last visitors.

Lavinia Spencer became one of Elizabeth's earliest ladies-in-waiting and went on to marry not a sailor but Lord Annaly, who won the Military Cross while serving with the 11th Hussars during the First World War. She was to prove a loyal friend to Elizabeth and Bertie during the abdication crisis in 1936. According to her daughter, the Hon. Mrs Osborne King, 'When the storm broke it was to my mother that they turned. She was very much involved and used to go down a lot to visit them. Although she was gentle, she had an inner strength and was full of confidence. She always expressed her views with great honesty and was not afraid of calling a spade a spade. She was also very discreet.'

During the Second World War, Lavinia again displayed the *sang froid* which she had shown during the Zeppelin raids when she chauffeured General de Gaulle during the blitz. Elizabeth is godmother to Lavinia's daughter and The Queen is godmother to her granddaughter, also named Lavinia.

Katharine Hamilton went on to serve as a courtier for over fifty years, first as lady-in-waiting to Queen Mary and then, when Elizabeth became Queen, as her Woman of the Bedchamber. It was through the Royal Houshold that she met her husband, Reginald Seymour, who was an equerry to King George V. Described by many as 'a saint', Katharine had a strong sense of duty and, despite her privileged and sheltered upbringing, became a prison visitor. However, the sense of fun she shared with the other Mad Hatters did not desert her. Her stepson recalls that 'She and Queen Elizabeth used to have a particularly jolly time at Goodwood races.'

When the Mad Hatters were all debutantes together, they would often be invited to the same house-parties. No doubt their conversation as they prepared for the evening was as racy as their correspondence, but the larks that took place on such occasions were innocuous. Elizabeth's dresser Mabel Monty recalls one such scene at Glamis:

> The best way you could describe the ladies' landing was bedlam. They were out to enjoy themselves and there was a lot of teasing and practical jokes. I remember that they once persuaded the housemaids to sneak down to the gentlemen's quarters and put sprigs of holly in their beds. You can imagine the reaction. You could hear the screeching and laughter miles away.

Mabel Monty was obviously a beady-eyed (and beady-eared) observer of everything that happened within the vicinity of her young mistress,

In 1917 Elizabeth was driving a carriage and four when the horses took fright and bolted. Disaster was only narrowly averted and the next driving lessons that Elizabeth took were behind the wheel of a car

In the garden with Betty Cator, suitably mad-hatted

Lady Helen Cecil, Lady Doris
Gordon-Lennox and
Lady Katharine Hamilton

who was just three years older than herself. She was a housemaid at Glamis when Elizabeth was in her teens, rising to become one of her lady's maids and dressers. These days she lives in an old people's home on the coast just outside Dundee, a sharp-faced and canny ninety-four-year-old. She is always immaculately dressed in a starched blouse with a brooch at her throat, immensely proud to show off the royal mementos in her neat room – which include a china cat given to her as a needlework prize by Queen Mary. By an extraordinary coincidence, she married a Mr Stringer, a Special Branch officer, who had grown up on the Sandringham estate and used to play football with the young princes David and Bertie. Her memory today is as sharp as the holly sprigs secreted in those young gentlemen's beds.

A typical gathering of Mad Hatters on the night of a dance at Glamis might include Lady Katharine Hamilton, Diamond Hardinge,

Katharine McEwen, Lady Doris Gordon-Lennox, Hilda Blackburn, Bettine Malcolm, Grisell Cochrane-Baillie and, of course, Lady Lavinia Spencer, unless she were recovering from another hunting mishap. Young Mabel Monty, busily helping Lady Elizabeth into her latest change of clothes, observed their antics with pleasure:

> A lot of time was spent trying to decide what to wear for dinner and the girls nipped in and out of each other's rooms comparing notes. Everyone in turn tried on any number of dresses and then rejected the lot. There was a great deal of conspiracy and consultation before a final decision was made. They had the most lovely clothes, mostly handmade, and any one of them would have done well.
>
> There was hot competition for the one bathroom on the landing. They would queue up and shout at each other through the door, 'Why are you taking so much trouble – who's it *for?*'

That, of course, was always the big question. For Elizabeth it was harder than for most of her contemporaries: from the moment she was officially launched into society, in the summer of 1919, she was spoilt for choice. Suitors surrounded her. The giddy Mad Hatter had evolved into one of the most desirable debutantes of her day.

CHAPTER SIX

Admiring circle

··· ✦ ···

THE END of the Great War was also the end of an era. The Edwardian way of life had gone, the modern age had begun. A whole generation of young men had been devastated, killed or maimed on the battlefields, and many of those who survived reacted to the horror they had witnessed by indulging in every available pleasure.

For Lady Elizabeth Bowes Lyon and her friends, the outbreak of peace was a signal to resume the old enjoyable routine. To the officers back from the front and the young women they had left behind, the end of the war did not mark the end of an era so much as the beginning of a party.

Flitting between Glamis, St Paul's Walden Bury and St James's Square, Elizabeth was a typical debutante of her day, the privations of the war years rapidly forgotten in the pleasures of the social whirl. Her friend Lady Rachel Cavendish evokes the giddy tempo of those post-war seasons:

> I had a marvellous time and did absolutely nothing except enjoy myself. In those days we were not brought up to think we had to learn how to earn our living and were quite unable to do anything useful. Looking back on it now, it seems a very selfish and indulgent life but at the time, it did not occur to me to do anything different. Sometimes I wonder how we spent our time but I was never bored or without anything to do for a moment.
>
> In London, I saw my friends, played tennis, very badly, sometimes golf, equally badly, went to house-parties every weekend which I enjoyed enormously, and went to dances five nights a week.

Elizabeth at that time was sweet-natured, pretty and almost as mischievous as she had been as a child. Very quickly she collected a train of admirers who sought her out at dances and plotted to be

Elizabeth at nineteen. 'Aunt Elizabeth had so many suitors that she really did not know which way to turn.'

invited to the same house-parties at weekends. The fairytale version of her life might have us believe that Lady Elizabeth Bowes Lyon would inevitably fall in love with and marry the young prince destined be the King of England. So it turned out, but there were many twists and turns along the way.

In September 1920, the guests assembled at Glamis for the annual Forfar County Ball. According to the visitors' book, a house-party of fourteen was staying at the castle for the occasion. All Elizabeth's unmarried girlfriends were given bedrooms on the same floor which the staff quickly christened the 'Mad Hatters' Landing' because of the ceaseless giggling and high spirits. It is not recorded in which wing the young men of the party were quartered, but since several of Elizabeth's most ardent admirers were among them the castle servants might just as aptly have nicknamed it the 'Lovers' Landing'.

On the night of the ball, the Strathmores and their guests were joined by neighbouring families accompanied by their own visitors, all adding to the throng of men hoping to seize a dance with Elizabeth. With her elfin features, deep blue eyes and dark brown hair, in the eyes of her male contemporaries she was the picture of well-bred desirability. She was also an accomplished and graceful dancer. Fortunately for her, these were still the days of the dance card, when a girl could make her choice of partner without seeming too offensive to those she rejected.

Looking back more than three-quarters of a century, it is hard to form a clear picture of the exact nature of an upper-class romance in those days. Our current habits are a poor guide to the mores of the young Elizabeth and her contemporaries. Young men both could and did enjoy all sorts of experiences by slipping off into the demi-monde of 'actresses' and rakish married women. Within their own social circle, certainly as far as the young ladies were concerned, the notion of routine pre-marital seduction was so rare as to be virtually unthinkable. The borderline between a minor flirtation and a full-scale love affair was blurred, but beyond a certain point a proposal became inevitable. In the circumstances, young men naturally hesitated to declare their intentions. The passionate feelings of Elizabeth's suitors may be undocumented, and remembered only in family anecdotes, but they should certainly not be underrated.

Despite all the repressed ardour, the prevailing impression of social life among these young aristocrats in the early 1920s remains one of mischievous innocence. 'On the night of the ball it was chaos up there,' remembers Mabel Monty. 'The ladies' maids were run off their feet fetching this and that. All the girls were anxious to look their very best and I don't wonder. Some of the most eligible bachelors in the country were there, including a royal prince. They were keen to catch his eye.'

Most of the visitors who had come up for the ball stayed a week or more at Glamis. For the serious wooer, life must have been difficult, since everyone was expected to join in the endless round of games and sporting activities. Tennis went on virtually non-stop. As soon as one flushed set of players came off the court for a glass of lemonade, there were other volunteers to replace them. Elizabeth was much in demand as a partner, not only from amorous motives but because she was a good player.

No sooner had a gentleman finished his game and begun to plot a solitary stroll with his young hostess than he would be whisked off to the cricket field. There was also the shooting, which was excellent. If the weather was fine, the ladies normally joined the menfolk on the moors for a picnic lunch, the subject of many a tweedy photograph. In the evenings, after dinner, the guests would play cards or gather for songs round the piano. Charades were a regular fixture of such house-parties. So were racy games of 'sardines', which provided a rare opportunity for private flirtation, all the more thrilling for taking place in the nooks and crannies of a haunted castle.

Which of the young men assembled for the Forfar County Ball was to capture Elizabeth's heart? Fortunately, Elizabeth's dance card for the ball has been preserved, lying undiscovered in her private archive at Glamis. It is reproduced on p. 113. The dance programmes for a large ball were specially printed and usually had a tiny pencil attached to them. Elizabeth's, as we can see, was full, although she seems to have had time to doodle some unflattering caricatures on the back. The supper dance was the one girls had to be particularly choosy about, since it was accepted that your partner would take you in to supper and have the privilege of remaining with you while it lasted. Who this fortunate gentleman was on the night of the Forfar Ball is not clear but the card does provide evidence of which young gallants had tried hardest to take the floor with her – and, more significantly, which of them she had favoured.

On this particular evening Prince Paul of Serbia was fortunate enough to be chosen not only for a one-step called 'Courting', but for two waltzes, 'Appasionata' and 'Flattery'. Victor Cochrane-Baillie, however, must have been delighted with his total of four dances, including the romantically titled 'Lamp of Love' and 'Hold Me'. Lord Gage, after a fox trot called, significantly, 'I'm Tired of Second

Fiddle', reappears for a reel and and a one-step. Lord Doune had to settle for a fox trot and a one-step; and his brother, James Stuart, was the only one to partner Elizabeth for two consecutive dances, a fox trot and a reel.

It is difficult to gauge how seriously the twenty-year-old Elizabeth considered the courtship of her admirers, but evidence of the strength of their feelings occurs in the testimony of the sons of at least two of the young men at Glamis that night.

According to Prince Paul's son, Prince Alexander, who is now in his seventies and living in Paris, it has always been known in the family that his father was one of Lady Elizabeth's most earnest suitors before her engagement to the Duke of York. 'I have been told by various relations that my father was very keen on Elizabeth before her marriage and was one of her suitors. He was devoted to her for the rest of his life and even in times of trouble she was always his most faithful friend.'

Photographs of Prince Paul show a handsome, slightly saturnine man, obviously thoroughly at ease on the lawns of Glamis and St Paul's Walden Bury where he was a frequent visitor. One of Prince Paul's early stays at the castle was not so restful. For much of his young adulthood, the prince kept up an intense correspondence with his close male friend Jean, Comte de Ribes, then living in Paris. Hundreds of these letters have been kept by Paul's son, Prince Alexander, and have never been made public before. Many described visits to the Strathmore households. In this one he reveals a surprising despondency:

> I have been away for a week at Glamis where there was a large house-party of more than twenty people. It would have been great fun if I had been in a normal state of mind. Unfortunately that was not the case and I had some nasty moments. I had a fight with Doris Gordon-Lennox. I am afraid there is not much hope in that direction. Alas, I will try to forget. Life for me seems only to consist of a series of rebuttals.

This, it seems, was the point at which Paul began to turn his attentions to Elizabeth. The prince had known Lady Doris, the daughter of the Duke of Abercorn, since 1918 and had wooed her intermittently at parties and dances during the season. However, Doris was never very interested, and it was with some relief that she introduced him to her great friend Lady Elizabeth Bowes Lyon. Two weeks later he wrote of going with Elizabeth and her brother Michael to a 'very jolly' dinner party at Grosvenor House, given by Lord Dalkeith. The dinner preceded the Cazalet ball and he adds, 'It was great fun. London is very gay and we danced a lot.'

Forfar County Ball

8th September 1920

Elizabeth's dance card for the
Forfar County Ball,
8 September 1920

Programme.

1 FOX TROT. " I know where flies go."
2 ONE STEP. "Courting."
3 WALTZ. " Hawaiian Moonlight."
4 FOX TROT. " I'm tired of 2nd fiddle."
5 ONE STEP. "Irene."
6 WALTZ. "Appassionata."
7 FOX TROT. "The Russian Rag."
8 REEL.
9 WALTZ. "Lamp of Love."
10 ONE STEP. "El Rilicario."
11 FOX TROT. "Dardenella."
12 WALTZ. "Flattery."
13 ONE STEP. "Hold Me."
14 ONE STEP. "Chong."
15 FOX TROT. "Bidely."
16 REEL.
17 WALTZ. ": Love in Lilac time."
18 ONE STEP. "Swanee."
19 ONE STEP. "You'd be surprised."
20 WALTZ. "Oh, la la!"

Engagements.

1 Victor
2 Prince Paul
3 Mr McSween
4 Lord Gage
5 R. and Victor
6 Prince Paul
7 Mr McSween
8 Lord Gage
9 Victor
10 Lord Gage
11 Lord Doune
12 Prince Paul
13 Victor
14 Lord Doune
15 James S.
16 James S.
17 Mr Don
18 vic
19 Murphy
20 Unknown

By March Elizabeth was visiting Paul at Oxford, where he was an undergraduate at Christ Church. 'Lady Nina Balfour came to spend the day here with five beauties including Elizabeth Lyon. It was delicious to see them and we had a very jolly time. Elizabeth was in marvellous form and very funny,' he writes to his friend Jean. Then it was off to the Christ Church ball and yet more dancing. Paul and Elizabeth were together again in June when they stayed with Captain and Lady Nina Balfour at Bisham Abbey for Ascot. The romantic nature of these settings and occasions may well have led contemporaries to conclude that the young couple's friendship had by now proceeded well beyond the stage of mere flirtation.

Prince Paul had led a nomadic and tragic life. Born in St Petersburg on 15 April 1893, he was the only child of Prince Arsène Karageorgevic of Serbia and Aurore Demidoff, Princess of San Donato. Prince Paul's mother came from an immensely wealthy family whose fortune had been founded by a chance encounter between a poor blacksmith and the Tsar, Peter the Great. The upshot of the meeting was that the blacksmith set up a munitions factory and during Russia's war with Sweden earned not only a great deal of money but the title of count. Further shrewd marriages brought the family into high society; through his mother's brothers Paul inherited much of his early interest in classical art as well as a magnificent villa in Rome and financial independence. According to his former son-in-law and biographer Neil Balfour, nephew of the prince's great university friend Christopher Balfour, 'Why Arsène and Aurore ever married remains a mystery. His temperament and background made him a wholly unsuitable husband, while Aurore was clearly unequal to her responsibilities as a mother. They were a profoundly unhappy couple and they did not remain together for long.'

Prince Alexander says:

> My father had a very tough childhood because he was abandoned by his mother and his father. His father was only interested in fighting wars and duels. He fought twelve duels in his life and won them all because he was a crack shot. He also loved war and fought in nine of them. That he was such a restless and warlike character is no wonder, given that he was the grandson of the legendary Kara Djorje, Black George, the dark-faced swineherd who led a rebellion against Serbia's hated Turkish rulers and became the undisputed ruler of the country. Paul's mother, I'm afraid, who felt her husband had deserted her to do all this fighting and shooting, ran off with an Italian gentleman.

Prince Paul left Russia with his mother and a nurse when he was one, and settled in Nice. Aurore could not wait to be free of her son and

The Prince punting on the
Isis. His friend Comte Jean de
Ribes is seated on the left;
their companion is identified
only as George

'I had a fight with Doris
Gordon-Lennox. I am afraid
there is not much hope in
that direction'

Prince Paul at Oxford, 1914;
his first taste of happiness

persuaded Arsène's eldest brother to bring him up. According to Neil Balfour:

> From the day that Paul left Nice with his nurse and his few belongings, he was to see his mother again only twice. As an old man he would tell how he could remember his mother from only two brief but emotional encounters. Once, aged about six, he was taken out to a large cruise ship on Lake Geneva where a lady clasped him to her bosom for what seemed an eternity, and in his tiny heart an eternity of bliss, and then introduced him to her friends as her son.
>
> Then again, aged perhaps eight, he was taken late one evening in the middle of winter to a station where he was told to wait. Presently a train pulled up and the same lady stepped off, hugged her son for some minutes, then, tears streaming down her cheeks, got on the train again and sped away.

His father, brash, unthinking and extrovert, also had no time for his timid and affectionate son. At the age of seven, the prince lost the only person who had ever shown him any love when his nurse was dismissed. He was sent to boarding school in Lausanne which was cold, bleak and infested with rats. There he was to stay for the next four years. 'He told me there were rats crawling round his room,' says Prince Alexander, 'and for the rest of his life, if he saw a rat or a mouse, he would shriek with terror.'

In June 1903, news arrived from Serbia that the King and Queen had been assassinated, hacked to pieces in a closet, and that Paul's uncle Peter was to succeed as monarch. For the next nine years Paul was brought up in the rigid confines of the court in Belgrade, persecuted by his sadistic and mentally unbalanced cousin, Prince George. This odious youth tried to drown Paul and fired live bullets at his feet to make him jump. Much to everyone's relief, Paul came up with a solution to his unhappiness: he announced that he wished to finish his education at Oxford University and in the spring of 1913 he went up to Christ Church to read classics.

Balfour writes of this period:

> For Paul arrival at Oxford was like a dawn – an awakening which was to shape his mind, his character and attitudes for life. For the first time he found himself free from constraint and among contemporaries who shared his tastes, who gave him the affection of which he had been deprived and who introduced him to a world full of confidence and youthful enthusiasm.

The war interrupted this idyll. At the outbreak of hostilities he returned to Serbia to find the country in chaos. The Austrians were

116

attacking from all sides and by the end of November the Serbian royal family were forced to evacuate Belgrade. The appalling privations and difficulties which followed caused lifelong damage to Paul's health. Eventually, however, the war was over and he was able to return to Oxford to take up his former way of life, complete with car, manservant and a flat in London.

He enjoyed the long round of dinner parties, balls, house-parties and long lunches. To Jean he wrote again, 'Lunched at a new club called Bucks. It is the rendezvous of young elegant society. The house belongs to Lord Anglesey and the French chef is remarkable.' Paul was much in demand and confessed to Jean that he was dreading his final exams. 'I have had to turn down all invitations for the present,' he wrote. He took his Oxford finals in 1920 and passed with distinction.

During his last year at university the prince's relationship with the young Bowes Lyons became even closer when Elizabeth's elder brother moved in with him. 'I hope to be back at Oxford on 10 October,' he wrote to Jean. 'Michael Lyon is coming to live with me in Lord Apsley's place. Ivor Churchill is also moving in.'

The friendship with Michael naturally brought the prince and Lady Elizabeth together more frequently, as they shared outings and trips to the theatre. Paul was not only an enthusiastic opera fan and ballet-goer; he also loved the music hall. So, of course, did Elizabeth and we know the title of at least one show they went to see together: *Stop Flirting*.

Ironically Prince Paul also shared the Mayfair flat with one of his rivals for Elizabeth's affections, Lord 'Grubby' Gage. It was at this time that, according to Neil Balfour, the prince was seriously considering Lady Elizabeth as a possible bride. She was, he said, the prettiest girl in Britain 'with her shining, lively eyes and beautiful smile'.

She wrote to him from Paris in April 1921 while he was also abroad in Belgrade. He replied promptly. 'My dear Elizabeth,' he wrote in his clear, sloping hand:

> I can't tell you how touched I was to see that you haven't forgotten me yet – it really was very kind of you! I am afraid this will be a very dull letter as my life here is terribly monstrous ...
>
> I expect to leave Belgrade on May 21st, with my cousin Alexander, for Paris where we might arrive on Tuesday morning May 24th. I do hope that you will still be there as I am simply longing to see you again & also we might have some of our fast parties in the gay French metropolis ...
>
> I have been rather depressed lately but have decided to take life

With Katharine McEwen on the lake at St Paul's, where Michael nearly drowned

Michael, Betty Somerset and friends at Glamis

cheerfully in the future & to live more in the present than I did. In one word I shall become 'fast'.

Best love, Paul

For the time, this must be regarded as quite a racy letter from a royal prince to a commoner, however well-bred. In a postscript he begs her to call him Paul. Certainly, in the view of the servants at Glamis, marriage was in the air. 'Prince Paul was a great favourite of everyone's and got on marvellously with Lady Elizabeth's brothers. He was charming to everyone but especially to Lady Strathmore. He was keen to marry Lady Elizabeth and knew how influential her mother would be in the decision. He was obviously mad about her.'

Although Paul knew Prince Albert well, when the latter's engagement to Elizabeth was announced in January 1923 it took him by surprise. He wrote to Jean, 'What do you think of Elizabeth's engagement? I didn't expect it especially after my visit to Glamis in September when I was there with Bertie York.' In an age when even the most intimate friends seldom put their deeper emotions on paper and always maintained an air of insouciance about affairs of the heart, that phrase 'especially after my visit to Glamis' has a certain implication.

Nevertheless, the prince continues, 'I am delighted about the marriage for many reasons. Firstly for her, then for him and then for the country as she cannot fail to create an excellent impression in England and Elizabeth will not fail to charm the crowds.' He added sadly, 'My Queen of Yugoslavia is still missing and so I can't plan my future. When *will* it happen?'

The prince, who was now thirty, did not have long to wait. During the summer season of 1923, at a ball given by Lady Zia Wernher, he set eyes on Olga, the beautiful eldest daughter of Prince Nicholas of Greece. Although they were not introduced, he apparently stared at her for most of the evening and spent the rest of night scheming to see her again.

Olga had previously been engaged to Crown Prince Frederick of Denmark, but his feelings towards her cooled and the engagement was broken off. According to her son Prince Alexander, she had not been keen on him in the first place, thinking that he drank too much.

Her parents then hoped that she might catch the eye of the Prince of Wales. It was, by coincidence, in his company that Paul was first presented to his future wife. 'This was, as far as Olga was concerned, a major distraction,' says Neil Balfour. 'Probably Paul was already in love with her. From the very beginning, he had noted her beauty and innocence and conceived the wild notion that she might make a perfect wife.' The date was Tuesday, 10 July. A fortnight later they were at a ball together at Hurlingham. On the twenty-eighth, Paul asked Olga to the cinema and Neil Balfour tells the charming story of what happened next. 'He seemed unusually preoccupied and nervous. Olga, correctly sensing the mood, leant towards him and prompted in a whisper, "Have you found what you want?" Paul, who a few moments earlier had been consumed with apprehension and fear, turned to her and, with a look full of gratitude, said "Yes, at last!"'

Prince Paul's friendship with Elizabeth continued throughout his life. Olga's sister Marina married Elizabeth's brother-in-law, the Duke of Kent; Prince Albert was not only Prince Paul's best man but godfather to his eldest son, Prince Alexander. When the baby was born, the couple were staying at White Lodge in Richmond Park, lent to them by Elizabeth, then Duchess of York. It was to be the first of many such acts of kindness.

After the assassination of his cousin King Alexander in October 1934, Paul was recalled to Serbia as Prince Regent, until the young King Peter came of age. Paul ran the country effectively until March 1941 when he was caught in a conflict of interests between his country and Britain. Winston Churchill had been pressing him to declare war on Germany, but he felt unable to do so, as Prince Alexander explains:

> England and France had steadfastly refused to sell Serbia any arms during the period between 1918 and 1940 and all the ammunition dated from 1914. Only one cartridge in six worked. They had no army and no weapons. My country would have been overrun in no time and there would have been a terrible loss of life.

Prince Paul therefore, after stalling for as long as he could, signed an appeasement treaty with the Italians and the Germans. One important clause, not disclosed until after the Second World War, stated that no German soldier would set foot on Balkan soil. Germany was preparing to attack Russia and had pressed hard for this treaty. Prince Paul had warned Britain of the danger but had been ignored by the Foreign Office. 'Prince Paul felt himself totally betrayed by Britain,' says Neil Balfour.

> In the years leading up to the war, he had carefully recorded the minutes of every cabinet meeting in Belgrade and warned of Germany's re-armament. He was a complete anglophile and saw it as his duty to pass on every scrap of information he could to the Foreign Office ... He was considered a hysterical aesthete and not to be taken seriously. Four days

after the *coup d'état* and just as he had predicted, the Germans had overrun his country.

His signing of the treaty led to a *coup d'état*, encouraged by Britain, and Prince Paul and his family were exiled to Kenya where they were put under house arrest for the duration of the war.

Britain's King and Queen, however, did not desert their old friend. According to Prince Alexander, 'The whole thing came to a head in 1942 when my uncle the Duke of Kent was killed in an air crash. My mother was allowed back to England to be with her sister, who was on the verge of collapse.' During her visit, Olga's dignity and discretion did much to restore Prince Paul's reputation. She had private meetings with the King at the Kents' country home, Coppins, and put her husband's side of the story. Thanks to the discreet intervention of Elizabeth and Bertie, Alexander was allowed to join the RAF and went on to serve with distinction in Bomber Command.

Shortly after the war, Prince Paul and Princess Olga were invited to continue their exile in relative comfort in South Africa. However, Paul remained despondent. He lay in a darkened room, his face turned to the wall, with a revolver under his pillow. 'He was threatening suicide and felt his life was at an end,' recalls Neil Balfour. At this point, Elizabeth arrived on a state visit to South Africa and took two hours out of her busy schedule to visit Paul. Balfour continues:

> No-one else was present at the meeting but when Paul emerged he was a changed man. The feeling is that Elizabeth had assured him that both herself and Bertie, not to mention all his English friends, thought him incapable of a treacherous act and gave him their full support. From then on he started to pick up the threads of his life and eventually made his home in Paris.

Whenever he visited London, he was always a welcome guest and often stayed with his loyal friend The Queen Mother at Clarence House.

Prince Paul was not the only young man to be dealt a blow by Elizabeth's engagement to Bertie York. One of her most eligible suitors was Viscount Gage, who inherited the title when he was seventeen, together with a magnificent Tudor mansion Firle Place set in the Sussex downs. He had met Elizabeth through her brother Michael when they were both undergraduates at Oxford.

His son, the present Lord Gage, now in his sixties, still lives at Firle. 'My father was the only boy among a family of sisters and as a child led a very sheltered life. His own father was frail and very religious and he was brought up under a very Victorian regime. His mother was a great hostess and loved to entertain German royalty, so he was brought up principally by nannies and governesses.'

Later he was sent to the preparatory school St Peter's, Seaford and then on to Eton, where he was two years younger than Elizabeth's brother Michael. Like the Bowes Lyon boys, he had a passion for cricket; he was also an excellent horseman and was to become popular with all the Strathmores. He was nineteen at the outbreak of the First World War and served with the future Prime Minister, Harold Macmillan, in the Sussex regiment. He was shot near the heart at Passchendaele and, according to his son, as he lost consciousness he heard his batman remark, 'He's a goner.' He survived but was not fit enough to rejoin his regiment until after the Armistice.

Life at Firle Place was never dull: just before the war the bohemian Bloomsbury set had moved into the vicinity, as did the economist Maynard Keynes. On one memorable occasion Duncan Grant, Vanessa Bell, her sister Virginia Woolf and several others dressed up and marched on Firle, claiming to be the old Lord Gage's illegitimate children. The present Lord Gage recalls: 'My grandfather was a saintly and totally moral man and the practical joke gave him quite a start. He had thought they were just some rather queerly dressed tenants coming to pay their respects.' His father viewed them with equal apprehension:

> He was very proud of them but also a little frightened, particularly when they pretended to mistake him for the plumber. It was a sort of love-hate relationship. He was very quick and always fascinated by new ideas but he rather disapproved of the lifestyle. He once described them as people who 'dwelt in squares (Bloomsbury) and lived in triangles (ménage à trois)'.

Although he entertained the Bloomsbury set, he preferred the company of Maynard Keynes with whom he frequently dined. 'It's a measure of his intelligence that he was able to keep his end up,' adds his son.

In 1920, in the company of Elizabeth's brother Michael, Lord Gage went up to Oxford to read agriculture. Rich, titled and with a magnificent mansion at his disposal, Lord Gage was a lavish host and Elizabeth was a regular visitor to Firle. She and Lord Gage had a common interest in music and both were avid readers. They also shared a passion for chocolate. However, what really brought them together was their similar sense of humour. 'He was a wag and so was she. My father used to give grand parties at Firle in the twenties and Lady Elizabeth was a frequent guest. There was definitely a romance,' says his son, but will not elaborate further. He saw The Queen Mother

122

An Oxford dining club in 1920. Lord Gage is seated second from the left in the front row, with Michael fourth from the left. Ivor Churchill is fourth from the right in the back row. The three shared digs together where Elizabeth was a regular visitor

'How is wonderful Firle?' Elizabeth at the Sussex home of Lord Gage.

Chips Channon, diarist and confidant of the aristocracy, in Bavarian dress. He was to write in his diary, 'Gage is desperately fond of Elizabeth'

The Ogilvy brothers: Their mother, Lady Airlie, and Lady Strathmore both thought that Joseph and Elizabeth would make a good match, until his brother Bruce fell for her. Joseph is at the wheel and Bruce is standing on the dashboard. Also standing in the front is Diamond Hardinge, who died tragically young of tuberculosis

After dinner at Glamis. Arthur Penn is on Elizabeth's right. Seconds later Elizabeth covered her ears with cushions because of the bagpipe-playing recently. 'When I met her she said to me, "How is wonderful Firle?" She still has fond memories of the place.'

In January 1922, a few days before Elizabeth's engagement to the Duke of York was announced, the diarist Chips Channon noted: 'Poor Gage is desperately fond of her - in vain, for he is far too heavy, too Tudor and squirearchal for so rare and patrician a creature as Elizabeth.'

Lord Gage did not marry until eight years after Elizabeth's wedding.

In the Second World War, Lord Gage, although by now forty-five years old years old, re-joined the army as a captain, choosing the Coldstream Guards as his regiment. He served with great gallantry and it was generally believed that he was involved in counter-espionage operations, although he never amitted it. He is remembered by Lord Longford as reserved, dignified and humorous, while Lord Hailsham recalls him as a highly intelligent and popular man who kept himself to himself. His son admits that his father found it difficult to communicate. 'He didn't like too much intimacy. He hated signs of physical love in films. It embarrassed him.'

The viscount is probably best remembered for his quip during the debate in the House of Lords on *Lady Chatterley's Lover*. 'Would you show this book to your wife?' asked one of his fellow peers, to which Lord Gage replied, 'I would certainly show it to my wife – not to my gamekeeper.' His other claim to fame is also characteristic. 'My father was once riding in a point to point and his cap fell off,' recalls his son. 'He stopped, dismounted and picked it up before resuming the race.'

Lord Gage had two distinct advantages as a suitor, besides his *sang froid* in the saddle and sharing with Elizabeth's father a mania for doing crosswords. He was a great friend of her brothers and was often invited to parties at Glamis for the shooting. He was also a rich man. 'My father was always pleading poverty,' says his son, 'but he in fact he was very well off.'

He and Elizabeth remained close friends. They saw each other regularly until his death in 1982. 'He could pop into Clarence House whenever he wanted, unannounced, and Queen Elizabeth was always delighted to see him,' says his butler, who is still in service at Firle Place.

According to Mrs Alice Winn, a neighbour of the Strathmores in St James's Square, Elizabeth had far more suitors than Prince Paul and Lord Gage from whom to choose. Mrs Winn was a niece of Nancy Astor, the American who had married into the wealthy Astor family and became Britain's first woman Member of Parliament. Showing a sharp understanding of modern times, Mrs Winn says:

> Lady Elizabeth was what, today, we would call an 'It' girl. She had a stream of suitors and was the toast of debutante society. Unlike me, she had the ability to listen and make everyone she met feel special. The men returning from the horrors of the First War found her irresistible. She offered the warmth and comfort they had lacked for so many years and everybody was mad about her.
>
> My parents were dead by the time I came out and my aunt was busy in the House of Commons, so I was given my own car and chauffeur. As I lived next door to Elizabeth, I used to give her lifts to all the dances. She was hardly through the door before young men were queuing to speak to her.

Elizabeth's niece, Lady Mary Clayton, confirms this view. 'Aunt Elizabeth had so many suitors that she really did not know which way to turn. Granny gave up after my mother Rosie had turned down two dozen proposals of marriage. It was much the same with Aunt Elizabeth.'

The list of Elizabeth's admirers included Freddie Dalrymple-Hamilton, who had earlier been in love with her elder sister Rosie and seems to have had a crush on the whole Strathmore family; and the Hon. Bruce Ogilvy, younger son of the Earl of Airlie. When Elizabeth was still a young girl, her mother had discussed with her close friend and neighbour, the Dowager Countess of Airlie, the possibility of linking their two families by marriage. Blanche, Lady Airlie was a frequent correspondent and always enquired tenderly about the countess's youngest daughter. 'How is Elizabeth?' she writes. 'Still as fascinating as ever I'm sure. I hope her prince will come along soon.' At first, the eldest son Joe, known as Dit, was thought the most suitable match but, as the years progressed, it became apparent that his younger brother Bruce was more interested in Elizabeth. He often wrote amusing, affectionate letters, teased her about flirting with other admirers and took her out for drives in his car. According to the present Lady Airlie, Bruce was extremely attractive with wavy hair and dark eyes. 'He had great *joie de vivre* and was a real lady-killer. He was the most enormous fun to be with,' says the countess. 'He was terribly charming and fantastic with people. He was totally classless and would make friends with anybody.'

Bruce had something of a wild streak: he used to play the ukelele and sing along to it as he danced on table tops. He was also extremely brave, winning the Military Cross during the First World War. 'Uncle Brucie was certainly very keen on Lady Elizabeth,' says the present Lady Airlie. 'He was definitely one of her many suitors and for a while

126

they had a little romance. He continued to admire her until the day he died.'

A more serious suitor was Sir Arthur Penn, fourteen years her senior and a close friend of her brothers. Lady Penn, his nephew's widow, says that Sir Arthur 'was absolutely devoted to her throughout his life. He adored her.'

Educated at Eton, he was the grandson of the famous marine engineer John Penn. Sir Arthur was a colourful character, who went into battle during the First World War waving a cigarette in one hand and the family's ancestral sword in the other. He returned a war hero, having won both the Military Cross and the Croix de Guerre. He qualified and practised as a barrister, then went into the City, working for a large bill-broking firm where he became company chairman. He is remembered for his great kindness and the way in which he would put even the most nervous at their ease. He had a lifelong interest in the arts and was himself highly gifted. A witty cartoonist, he invariably made his own Christmas cards. Lady Penn recalls that, 'Children loved him because he had a marvellous sense of the ridiculous.'

Sir Arthur was one of Lady Elizabeth's most trusted friends, both before and after her marriage. It was to him that she turned when trying to make up her mind whether to accept Bertie's proposal, and the three of them often appeared together in photographs. In 1937 he joined the royal household as treasurer.

After King George VI died in 1952 there was widespread speculation that Elizabeth would marry her long-standing admirer. 'Arthur was horrified and upset by the reports,' says Lady Penn. 'There was no truth in them.'

However, the rumours persisted and eight years later, The Queen Mother's spokesmen were still describing them as nonsense. Clearly there were those who remembered how Arthur Penn had doted on the young Elizabeth Bowes Lyon and firmly believed he doted still.

More than Arthur Penn, however, or Lord Gage or Prince Paul, there was one man who in September 1920 was to occupy Elizabeth's thoughts. He was well-born, handsome, charming and brave and he was the man who had claimed her for two consecutive dances at the Forfar County Ball: his name was James Stuart.

CHAPTER SEVEN

The great love?

· · · ❖ · · ·

THE HON. JAMES Gray Stuart came from one of the oldest and noblest families in Scotland. His father became the seventeenth Earl of Moray. His ancestor was the elder half-brother of Mary Queen of Scots, the bastard son of King James V, who acted as Regent until Mary came of age. He was known as 'The Good Lord James'. In *The Queen and the Hive*, Edith Sitwell said of him: 'Although Mary was Queen, it was that most remarkable man, James Stuart, her elder half-brother, who was in all but name ruler of Scotland,' adding: 'It was his misfortune and Scotland's that he was not King.'

The Good Lord James's abilities were passed on to succeeding generations. Stuarts distinguished themselves in the public arena, serving King and country in one high office after another. The young James kept up the family traditions. He won the Military Cross and Bar during the First World War. At twenty-six he entered the House of Commons as Member of Parliament for Moray and Nairn. He went on to become Winston Churchill's Chief Whip, Secretary of State for Scotland and a Companion of Honour before being created Viscount Stuart of Findhorn for his long and faithful service.

He also had a reputation as the most notorious philanderer of his generation.

James was born in Edinburgh on 9 February 1897. His mother Edith was the daughter of a rear-admiral. Like his elder brothers Francis and John and his little sister Hermione, James had the typical upbringing of a well-bred child in the late Victorian era. Nurse was an all-important figure in the little boy's life; even when he had gone away to war he continued to write to her from the trenches. But his parents were less remote than was often the case in those days. 'My father had a very happy childhood,' says his daughter the Hon.

James, looking every inch the debonair bachelor

Davina Ritchie. 'They were a close-knit family and made their own fun. He was particularly close to his brother John, and so it remained for the rest of their lives. Wherever my father was to be found, John was never far away.'

James's father succeeded to the earldom the year of Queen Victoria's death, 1901, when his little son was four years old, and so added two great estates to Doune Lodge, the home they already owned in Scotland. These estates were Darnaway in Moray and Kinfauns in Perthshire, close to the Bowes Lyon stronghold at Glamis. James and his brothers learnt to fish, shoot and ride, though the sport he himself most enjoyed was golf in which he became an excellent player.

When he was nine, James was sent to a preparatory school in Dorset before following his eldest brother, Francis, to Eton in January 1910. Clearly he had not worked hard enough in the preceding four years because as he explains in his autobiography, *Within the Fringe*, 'I was said to have done poorly at my Common Entrance examination but I had my first "little bit of luck" when at the end of my first half my sensible form-master, the late George Lyttelton, saw to it that I got a "double remove" although I was absent with the measles.'

Having skipped a form, James settled down to enjoy himself and make a success of his schooldays. Although not academically brilliant, he was quick and alert and found no difficulty with his lessons. He became a 'wet-bob', rowing in his house VIII. On that most famous of parents' days, the Fourth of June, he and his fellow oarsmen paraded down the Thames in their flower-decked straw boaters and managed to avoid capsizing as they stood up in their narrow craft, raising their blades in the traditional salute.

It is very likely that Lady Elizabeth Bowes Lyon witnessed this display since both her brothers nearest to her in age – David, twenty-one months her junior and Michael, seven years older than herself – were at Eton. She rarely missed an opportunity to visit the school – least of all this annual gathering of the Etonian tribes to picnic and gossip on Agar's Plough.

By the summer of 1914, James had reached the sixth form. He had also been elected to Pop, most exclusive of Eton societies, whose members are given the privilege of wearing outlandish waistcoats and spongebag trousers. His progress in the college Officer Training Corps, which was taken very seriously in those pre-war days, was less impressive. He did not get beyond the rank of private and was a source of extreme exasperation to the company commander, who was also his mathematics master. As if James's academic performance were not bad enough, reported this master, 'What is more important than Stuart's mathematics is the fact that he will be Head of House next half and he is so inefficient that I cannot possibly make him a lance-corporal in the Corps.'

Luckily for James, his father had a low opinion of schoolmasters and handed his sons the school reports to read for their own amusement. When he heard that his youngest son had received a severe punishment for breaking a minor rule, his sole comment was, 'Your housemaster must be a fool.'

James was at summer camp with the Officer Training Corps at Tidworth when war was declared and he decided to 'bunk' school - Etonian slang for quitting the place. 'Although my name appears in the school list, it is followed by the letters ABS because I had joined the Army. So I missed my last year at Eton and the whole time I should have spent as my father intended at Trinity, Cambridge,' he reveals in his autobiography.

> My getting into the Army was without parental consent. My father, a stern man, ordered me to return to Eton but I won my first battle with him by explaining that I had orders to join the Royal Scots at Weymouth on September 15 and that I would be court-martialled if I failed to report.
>
> It is unlikely that this would have happened, as I was five months under age for the Army anyhow. My father had grounds for annoyance. I had been disobedient, and also no doubt he felt entitled to discourage me from courting an early death. It is also possible that, since no notice had been given to the school authorities of premature departure from Eton, he was annoyed at having to pay school fees for an absent son.

The decision was swiftly acted upon. James and a number of like-minded friends escaped from Tidworth and headed for London, only stopping *en route* at Eton to pick up their civilian clothes. They were determined to get 'lit up' and began the process with a very festive lunch. Michael Bowes Lyon, who was four years older than James and had left Eton for Oxford some years previously, was one of the party. The story is told in the Strathmore family that James and Michael got so 'lit up' that when they eventually headed off with the intention of joining the Black Watch, they took a wrong turning and ended up enlisting in the Royal Scots by mistake. The Stuart family, however, explain the choice of regiment by saying that James was desperately ashamed of his knobbly knees and preferred wearing tartan trews to a kilt.

Whatever the reason, James's autobiography recalls that the celebrations were prolonged and hilarious:

The wet bobs practising in the shadow of Windsor Castle. James was particularly proud of his prowess on the river

Eton, the Fourth of June. James is third from the right

132

I remember Tim [Nugent] and I ended up in the old Monico at Piccadilly Circus where there were some Frenchmen and where we all got very excited, shaking hands madly and assuring one another that, together with the glorious French army, we would walk through the Germans in no time. There appeared to be no doubt that Berlin and victory could not take more than six weeks and our sole problem was how to get out there before victory was complete.

When the band struck up the 'Marseillaise' we all stood up and shook hands again. Then a British party started to sing 'It's a long way to Tipperary' and we all had to stand up again and clasp hands because the French thought it was our National Anthem.

James duly joined his battalion at Weymouth on 15 September 1914, 'happy to find a number of good friends from both Scotland and Eton among my comrades', Michael of course being one of them. The two young men shared their first taste of Army life together. As the elder, Michael took the seventeen-year-old James under his wing and kept a watchful eye on him.

'We were under canvas on a cricket field,' James wrote, 'and it was a healthy and happy enough life, with physical training, drilling, route-marching twelve or fourteen miles round Portland Bill to harden the feet, and occasional off-duty evenings in Weymouth.'

The nights out in Weymouth were the young men's initiation into adult life. The pubs were crowded, the beer flowed, and the town was nightly invaded by country girls looking for a good time. 'The atmosphere was chaotic,' James reminisced:

with people rushing here and there, making last minute purchases of things they thought they needed but had forgotten to buy before; stocking up on chocolate and razors and cigarettes before setting out for the evening, determined to enjoy themselves and make the most of their last days of freedom before they were dispatched to France from Southampton.

The restaurants were packed and so were the public houses. There were pretty girls everywhere only too glad to take a soldier's arm and have fun while the going was good. A mood of patriotism, enthusiasm and confidence pervaded everywhere. The only anxiety being that we wouldn't get there soon enough and miss the 'show'.

They need not have worried. They got there quite soon enough. James and Michael were quickly disillusioned, faced with heavy fighting on the front line and bogged down in the appalling grind of trench warfare. But the friendship forged in the heady days of preparing for war was to be a lasting one.

James was to prove a fine soldier. The schoolboy optimism of the new recruit vanished as the mud of the Belgian battlefields rose above his boots. So bad were conditions that the time a man spent in the trenches soon had to be halved. Regular soldiers, newly arrived from India, succumbed to frostbite and fell sick in their hundreds. James saw front-line action at Dickebusch. Then, a few days before his eighteenth birthday, he too fell ill and was invalided home. It was to be another thirteen months before he was fit enough to rejoin the regiment. When he returned to his battalion, in April 1916, he found it occupying precisely the same part of the line as when he had left it.

Soon James and his men were moved to the Somme. There he witnessed the terrible slaughter of the British push to capture High Wood and the last cavalry charge of the battle, when men and horses were mown down by machine-gun fire as they attempted to overcome the enemy's barbed wire defences.

Much of his time was spent on daring lone night patrols in No-Man's-Land, 'unarmed, as usual, because I couldn't be bothered carrying arms and was sure the game would be up anyway if I met the enemy.' In his autobiography he recalls one of these forays:

> One night when I was in front visiting my forward posts I ventured into High Wood and, hearing no movement or voices, went on to the far side of the wood about 600 yards beyond our own front line. I was able to report back that the place could be had for the asking, but nothing was done and not long afterwards the Germans reoccupied it and fighting was still going on for its possession weeks later.

He also tells the story of a brigade major who ignored his advice and insisted on reconnoitring the terrain ahead:

> I told him he could go no further and that if he tried he would almost certainly be killed. However, he again insisted and we parted company. Soon I heard the usual burst of fire and he was never again seen alive. He was awarded a posthumous Victoria Cross – but what did this and similar such acts achieve? Nothing but the waste of good life.

On another occasion James came close to wasting his own even more pointlessly, when he was nearly shot by one of his sentries: he had picked up a German helmet and, unthinkingly, put it on his own head.

By the time he was nineteen, James had been made up to adjutant and won the Military Cross. He went on to serve with gallantry at Arras and the third battle of Ypres, where his battalion suffered fifty per cent casualties in the first forty-eight hours of the attack. He was recommended for a DSO but turned down because he was considered 'too young'. Subsequently, to his annoyance, he discovered that 'spoilt' fellow officers in the Brigade of Guards had been given the award at the same age. He received a bar to his MC instead and this recognition gave him more than normal satisfaction:

> It gave me self-confidence. Having survived the battle of the Somme, I felt for a long time that I could weather anything. This valuable internal sense stayed with me for the next eighteen months and it was not until early 1918 that it began to weaken. I was by then too tired, and at the same time I began to feel that my luck in remaining alive and unwounded couldn't hold out much longer.

Later he adds: 'It is curious that as soon as a man's nerve gives way he is liable to die quite soon, and he seems to know it.' James cites two examples of this. One was a company commander called Berry who handed him a letter and small parcel for his mother hours before battle and told him that he knew he would not survive. 'I said the usual things about not being silly and we all had the same chance, but he was adamant. He was dead within twenty minutes of zero hour.' The other was a young subaltern called Palmer who suddenly handed over his revolver to his company sergeant-major whilst lying in a shell hole twenty yards from the German position. 'You have this. I won't want it any more,' he said and within ten minutes he was dead.

Luckily for James, his nerve held until the Armistice. This probably owed much to the breeziness of his character. Few First World War officers could have deserted – a firing squad offence – and got away with it. James did. It happened when he and his men were being transported to a new base camp at Etaples. The debonair young officer bribed the engine driver to stop briefly at a station *en route*. He then persuaded his commanding officer to take some rest, assuring him that he would see to it none of the men on board left the troop train. He hopped off himself and spent a comfortable night in a decent officers' club in Doullens. Challenged as to why he was two days late back from leave, James explained to his divisional commander that the idea of arriving at the depot with 2,000 disorganised men ('all total strangers to me'), was just 'too boring'.

The combination of charm and insolence worked. 'Well, Stuart,' said Major-General Deverell, 'as you deserted towards the enemy and not in the opposite direction, I think it may be overlooked on this occasion.' Not long afterwards the war ended and James was at Buckingham Place, receiving his gallantry awards from the the King.

James Stuart's war, though as hellish as every other soldier's, had had its moments of relief. Apart from his night of illicit luxury as a deserter in France, there had been weeks of leave in both London and

Paris. In later years he became known as a notorious rake, yet the young officer seems to have spent his furloughs in fairly decorous fashion.

In London, one of the great attractions was the music hall, which enjoyed a crescendo of popularity during the war years. Soldiers on leave formed a large and enthusiastic part of the audiences, James and his fellow officers occasionally among them. They went to see Stanley Holloway, Harry Lauder and not least Miss Gwendoline Brogden whose celebrated rendering of a well-known wartime song regularly brought the house down:

On Sunday I walk out with a soldier,
On Monday I'm taken by a Tar.
On Tuesday I'm out with a baby Boy Scout,
On Wednesday a Hussar;
On Thursday I gang oot wi' a Scottie,
On Friday, the Captain of the crew,
But on Saturday I'm willing,
If you'll only take the shilling,
To make a man of any one of you.

It was at the music hall one evening while he was home on leave that James Stuart met Elizabeth Bowes Lyon for the first time. This form of entertainment was very popular during the war years as Londoners high and low sought a sentimental, irreverent, risqué antidote to the horror of death across the Channel. It was therefore not as surprising as it might seem that members of two of the grandest Scottish clans should literally bump into each other in a such a cheerfully vulgar venue. Elizabeth and some of her family, including her brother Michael, were hurrying to their box when they encountered an oncoming party. In the ensuing confusion Michael spotted James and naturally introduced his brother officer to his attractive younger sister. Elizabeth did not see James again until after the war.

James's wartime leaves also included a visit to Paris where he met an old acquaintance. He had had a great crush on the actress Zena Dare since he had met her as a sixteen-year-old schoolboy at Eton. 'She came to tea with me, bringing, to my regret, her father-in-law, Lord Esher. It was like the old music-hall song "And her mother came too".' He was twenty when he met her again in Paris but the handsome young officer was over-awed. 'Once she let me drive her out to Versailles on a lovely afternoon, my first visit to that great monument of French civilisation; but I was far too shy of so beautiful a celebrity and I don't suppose I even opened my trap,' he recalls.

After the Armistice on 11 November 1918, and before he returned home to launch his career, James was stranded in Brussels for four months awaiting demobilisation. He arrived in the city in time for New Year's Day 1919 and set about painting the town red. 'I found a couple of pipers and took them into a smart restaurant and night club called the Merry Grill. This caused quite a stir and certainly woke the place up,' he recalls in his autobiography.

> We had a lot of fun in Brussels and I grew to love the place. The small restaurants provided excellent food and Burgundy, but it was expensive and I soon found to my horror that in a few weeks I had spent all my war savings for four years. However, as Winston Churchill once remarked to me, 'What is money made for except to spend?' (I had been com-miserating with him over the loss of a large sum of money in the American slump of 1929 and all he said was – 'Yes, how much better if I had spent it.')

While James was kicking his heels in Brussels, at home in Scotland his return was eagerly awaited by a young woman known to everyone as Elfie.

Evelyn Louise Finlayson was fifteen at the outbreak of the war, the beautiful daughter of a self-made Glasgow millionaire. She was the second of three sisters and apparently every man in Edinburgh would turn to admire her as she passed. 'This was very galling for Aunt Nell and Aunt Alix, whom no one noticed,' says her daughter Cynthia Munro.

Elfie and James first met when old Mr Finlayson bought a huge country mansion called Coldoch not far from Doune Lodge, one of the Stuart family's several homes. The three Stuart brothers were soon invited to tea and tennis and later asked to make up parties to local dances.

It was not only her beauty that set Elfie apart: she was literally head and shoulders above her contemporaries, being very tall for her generation. She played tennis well and gracefully. On the hunting field few could match her daring. She also rode astride rather than side-saddle, which was considered rather shocking in those days. She said she was forced to do so because of a back-injury. Whatever the truth, it undoubtedly attracted attention.

According to her daughter, 'Elfie was no intellectual, but she was sharp and very artistic – she drew and painted beautifully. She was acute and observant, a subtle, sophisticated woman. She had been carefully educated and spoke both French and German fluently.'

James and his eldest brother Francis were both very attracted to

Elfie, but James had an advantage: his birthday fell on 9 February and hers on 8 February, two years later. Joint parties were held either at one mansion or the other. Elfie was fêted up to midnight and James thereafter.

'They were thrown more and more together and other people increasingly commented what a good match they would make. In those days the young were very influenced by what people thought,' says her daughter.

James's father, who also had an eye for a pretty girl, thoroughly approved. 'I remember my mother telling me that Lord Moray fell ill during the war and she dressed up in her nurse's uniform and went to see him,' says Mrs Munro. 'She appeared at his bedroom door and said she was there to look after him. I asked her if she really meant it and she replied, "Of course not. I was only there to cheer him up." He wrote her many letters which I destroyed after her death because I thought they were rather improper.'

However, Elfie's most frequent correspondent was James, writing discreet but affectionate letters from Eton and more mature and intimate ones from the front. She was his sweetheart back home in Scotland and the thought of her kept him going during the darkest hours of battle.

'He was obviously very attracted to her and admired her a great deal. They were never allowed to say very much but, although the letters are circumspect, it is quite plain to see how fond they were of each other,' comments her daughter.

Finally demobilised, James hurried home to Elfie and a rapturous welcome. It was all the more delightful since, according to James's daughter Davina Ritchie, the home fires were not exactly blazing when he returned to Doune Lodge.

> After the horrors of this terrible war, which my father had survived by the skin of his teeth, he arrived home late at night. Although he had telegraphed ahead telling them that he was on his way, he was greeted only by the servants. He was told the family had gone to bed.
>
> At breakfast the next morning, his father looked briefly over his newspaper and remarked that he knew James must be back because he had left the hall light on. That was all that was said.

Francis, the heir to the earldom, proposed to Elfie. So did James. It was James, the third and youngest son, who was accepted. All seemed set fair. But, like so many other young men returning from the war, James had to think about earning a living. 'My father as the third son would stand to inherit nothing,' says his daughter. 'He was by no means well off and needed to earn money otherwise he wouldn't have

138

Evelyn Louise Finlayson,
'Elfie', whom James was
engaged to marry

James Stuart collecting
the Military Cross from
Buckingham Palace

James and John Stuart on the road from John O'Groats to Land's End

had a bean.' He had planned to return home from Brussels for a longish period 'as I thought I deserved a holiday and a rest after the rigours of the war'. But he had not been home long before he found himself being eased out of the family nest.

> My mother remarked, with studied casualness, that my father never liked to see any of us hanging about at home for more than three weeks at a time. It worried him to see us idle. So she advised that even if I had nothing in particular to do I should at least pretend to have some plan or occupation – in other words that I ought to remove myself for a time.
>
> My mother was a wise woman and I always took her advice if it was possible to do so. I didn't know what to do – or invent – but the problem was soon solved when our family solicitor arrived on a visit. I am sure my mother briefed him in advance, for he proceeded to propose that I might read for the Bar, which meant I would move to Edinburgh.

So James was despatched and dutifully began his studies, trudging up the Mound each morning from Prince's Street. However, although he managed to pass an exam in Public International Law and become apprenticed to a well-known firm of Edinburgh solicitors, Tods, Murray and Jameson, his marks were not good. His poor perfor-

140

At Coldoch, Elfie's home, in July 1919. Elfie is sitting between James (on her left) and his brother John. On the far right is Jean, a family friend

One of the many photographs duplicated in the albums of James and Elfie. Elfie's caption says it all

J.G.S. WORKING!

mance, after doing so well at school, worried him. 'But that did not prevent my enjoying golf at Muirfield or elsewhere at the weekends, and the social life of my native city.'

James also found time, during that summer of 1919, to visit Elfie at Coldoch. Their photograph albums show the engaged couple, happy and relaxed, in a variety of informal settings.

As a further distraction James and his brother John took up competitive motoring. Together with a third companion, a certain Captain Martyn, they took part in a race from John O'Groats to Land's End. It was a splendidly jolly affair. Photographs survive of the threesome posed proudly in front of their enormous, open-topped car waiting for the start and then shaking each other by the hand at journey's end. Just where James and his fellow drivers came in the race we do not know. It was an enthusiasm that was to continue for much of his life. Later, according to his daughter, he frequently took part in the London to Brighton run.

By the spring of 1920 it became depressingly clear that James's career in the law was going nowhere and that a serious decision about his future had to be made. Luckily a friend from his Brussels days, Louis Greig, came to the rescue: 'My brother John had known him in the Navy . . . He was also something of a hero, for he had been Scotland's rugby captain when I was a small schoolboy.' Louis Greig had gone to Brussels as private secretary to Prince Albert, who was representing King George V in the victory parade. He asked James if he could take Bertie under his wing and show him a good time. James was only too pleased to oblige. 'He was young and did not want to stay in the Palace all the time,' James recalls. 'Thus a few of us used to organise small parties and dances for the entertainment of the young prince. We had a great deal of fun and I got to know him quite well. What I did not know was that this meeting with Louis Greig, and hence with Prince Albert, was to prove a turning point in my life.' Evidently, James had made a good impression because he was asked by Louis to come to see him in London. And so, as James records, 'my whole life changed':

> Prince Albert had gone to Cambridge after the war and the suggestion was that I should join him there about a month before he came down and started his official career. I was to be his first equerry.
>
> Such a thought had never entered my head, but I was given little time to think. The pay was not big (£450 a year) but I would have my own bedroom in Buckingham Palace and would share a room to work in with Louis Greig. I would be given breakfast, and lunch any day I chose, and I could 'warn in' for dinner with the equerry on duty to the King if and when I wished.

142

After some consultation at home I replied that I would accept but that I could not do the job for long because of the need to earn more. The answer to this was that it was not worth starting if I was going to walk out at any moment, so we settled for a period of not less than one year and not more than two. I stayed for eighteen months.

The distractions of his new life put a strain on James's relationship with Elfie, although she remained a great favourite with his father. Lord Moray wrote a moving letter to his son's fiancée, which suggests that the account of his gruff greeting to James at the breakfast table gives an unfair picture of the earl:

I found a letter from James on my arrival here on Wednesday afternoon, being large and important and the contents were as important as the exterior. Something probably suggests to you to what I refer, so I need hardly weary you with an explanation. I was not surprised. It seemed only a natural sequence to what had gone before. As you have been to him as a Guardian Angel during these years of strenuous war – for which indeed I thank you from my inmost heart – so now if he would wish to be Your Guardian Angel for the future it seems only to be – provided you are agreeable to the conditions – naturally.

For as he said to me, when things were going badly out in France and everyone was disillusioned and discontented and out of spirits, he could not write to his mother or me, knowing quite well that we should feel the same and even more so – and so he turned to you – and you were willing to listen and gave him just the sympathy he needed ...

Of course it is quite impossible for us at home to realise or feel a fraction of what those who went through these years really felt or suffered. But that you helped in so large a measure to enable him to go through this ordeal is just that which I could never adequately thank you for. I should ever be in your debt. This last step which you have taken , although it does not discharge the debt, at any rate alters the circumstances ...

I will just say that I think you deserve one of the best and I cordially congratulate you for I know absolutely that you have gained one of the best: and I trust that both you and he may often in the future darken my doorstep.

The letter was written in August 1920. By November that same year, the engagement had been broken off. Elfie was heartbroken. Her daughter says:

I was told by my aunt and James's sister that it was he who had broken off the engagement. He realised he had rushed into an agreement he felt he simply did not want to go through with. The trouble with my mother was that she was fiendishly possessive and would have skinned him alive if she felt he had eyes for anyone else. She was probably the only girl he had

A house-party at St Paul's Walden Bury. Standing left to right: Lord Elphinstone (May's husband), Patrick, Lord Strathmore, Malcolm Lyon, James Stuart. Sitting, left to right: Elizabeth, Betty Cator, Dorothy, Lady Strathmore, May, Bettine Malcolm; Cecilia (the daughter of Patrick and Dorothy) is seated on the ground

James with Michael
at Glamis

Watching the rowing
on the Thames

ever got close to and he wanted to get around a bit. She wanted to tie him down and that is exactly what he did not want.

Elfie went off to Egypt to mend her broken heart but, by that time, James had another beauty in his sights: Lady Elizabeth Bowes Lyon.

While James had been poring over his law books, Elizabeth had been taking society by storm. The early part of 1919 found her in London where she watched President Wilson's triumphal drive through the city and witnessed the great ovation given to Marshal Foch. She saw the first post-war Lord Mayor's Show, with its lavish floats and brass bands, from the upstairs window of an office in the City. She joined in dozens of celebrations marking the allied victory.

At the end of April Elizabeth travelled to Northamptonshire to stay at Althrop: she was a bridesmaid at the wedding of her great friend Lady Lavinia Spencer. In May, June and July, she was in London for the season. Practically every night there was a dinner party followed by a dance. Occasionally a visit to the theatre broke the routine. All those hours of learning her dance steps from old Mr Neil paid off: she was voted the best dancer in town.

This was no small accolade since dancing was no longer the formal affair of years gone by. In the heady atmosphere of London after the First World War, dancing became a way of life. You could dance from luncheon through tea to dinner and on to breakfast time. Whilst you could never go out to dinner unchaperoned with a young man, to be in his arms doing the Twinkle, the Elfreda or the Shimmy morning, noon and night was perfectly acceptable.

As Elizabeth's friend Rachel Cavendish explains:

> The dances were very different from what they are now as you danced with your partner instead of alone or opposite him. The problem was to book them with people you wanted to dance with and to avoid the ones with whom you did not.
>
> It was made very clear to me by my aunts, the first time I was let loose in London by myself, that I was not to go anywhere alone with a man. None of my friends did either, so that was no hardship, although I once went to Kew on the top of a bus with someone and had a guilty conscience for weeks afterwards. There was no question of going to what were known as 'public' dancing places such as night clubs or restaurants. But that was no hardship either as we had plenty of dancing at other people's expense.

Elizabeth's Sundays were spent in Hertfordshire, recovering from the gaieties of the week before. Flirtations begun over the supper tables of the great hostesses were pursued amid the grounds and lakes of St

Paul's Walden Bury. When she had a spare moment Elizabeth would motor down to Eton to see her brother David, never forgetting to bring his favourite treat, an angel cake, as a welcome addition to tea.

Naturally she went to Ascot. She wore a white lace frock and a hat resembling a poke bonnet, a fact not missed by their old family friend Lord David Cecil. He noted that her fashion sense was picturesque, bordering on the eccentric.

That summer, the servants at Glamis were run off their feet as friends and family descended *en masse* for the shooting. Her great admirer Arthur Penn was one of the guests, as was her friend Betty Cator, one day to marry her brother Michael. Most guests stayed a week or a little longer, but a certain Michael Mosel-Isaacstein contrived to remain at Glamis from 1 August right through to 25 December.

Through his friendship with Michael, James Stuart also became a frequent guest at Glamis. His first entry in the visitors' book is for 24 September 1919, when, as one of the guests in a large house-party, he stayed ten days. 'My father and his brother James loved being invited to stay,' says the present Earl of Moray, John's son. 'Lady Strathmore was a wonderful and generous hostess and it was always the most tremendous fun. I think there was a good deal of larking about and high jinks as well as the cricket matches and the shooting. It was certainly much more fun than being at home. My father and uncle went regularly to Glamis.'

The 'Ramblings' of Lady Rachel Cavendish paint a grim picture of life at Kinfauns:

> One had to be on the dot for everything, clean and tidy, ready for grace before meals and be prepared for luncheon to take an hour and a half and dinner two hours. Lord Moray was a very slow eater and the dining-room chairs were lovely ladderback ones, but one of the rungs always got my back in the wrong place and I found them very uncomfortable after an hour or so.

Lord Moray, she says, was 'a tiny little man with very small feet; in fact, he could wear Lady Moray's shoes and I am sure she did not have big feet as she was like a bit of Dresden china, although quite tall. He always used a stick and shuffled about quite fast with very little steps. I never saw him cross or in a temper but he could be a tiger I believe.'

Lady Moray was apparently

> lovely looking and very gentle but determined in her way ... I used to think that her life must have been very dull as no one ever did anything.

> Every day was exactly the same as the last with a little walk in the morning and possibly a very gentle drive in the afternoon which used to send me to sleep ... I don't think anybody ever stayed with them except one friend of Lady Moray's who I don't think he liked at all but who he would just tolerate for her sake. I think she must have had a very difficult time with him, but she never showed it.

The only treat allowed was a picnic expedition to the Fishing House. 'It meant two cars going to the top of the hill above the river as in those days one could not drive down. One car was for us and the other for the butler and tea. It seemed to me quite extraordinary that there was so much fuss about taking tea out but there was. The butler even had his bowler hat on!'

The contrast between life at the Moray home and the warmth, excitement and informality of the Strathmore household must have been overwhelming. Hardly surprising, therefore, that James and John escaped whenever they could, driving between Kinfauns and Glamis in an open-topped Daimler.

At the time of James's first ten-day stay at Glamis, Lady Elizabeth was nineteen years old and had been presented at court at Holyroodhouse Palace during the King and Queen's summer stay in Edinburgh. James, three years older, was not only dashingly good-looking and famously charming; he was also something of a wag. 'He was always pulling someone's leg,' recalls Mabel Monty, her dresser. 'Lady Elizabeth loved nothing more than a bit of banter and so you can imagine the jokey, slightly flirty, conversations they had.'

James's daughter concurs:

> I think the reason that my father broke off his engagement to Elfie was that he was in a deep depression after the horrors of the First War and simply felt incapable of taking on a wife.
>
> Lady Elizabeth managed to bring him out of that depression and captured his heart. There is no doubt that they felt a great deal for each other.

As 1920 turned into 1921 and they attended the usual round of balls, dinner parties and country house weekends James continued his attentions to Elizabeth.

The couple talked and laughed non-stop when they were together and danced with each other whenever they could. James had a number of girlfriends besides Elfie (to whom he remained engaged until the autumn of 1920) and Elizabeth a string of admirers. But they looked so well together, everyone said. And they had so much in common. Both were highly attractive, she with her fashionable

148

daintiness, beautiful eyes, infectious laugh and devastating charm; he the debonair war hero with the devil-may-care poise and ready wit. Both came from ancient and distinguished Scottish families. Both were well educated by the standards of the times. They shared a sense of humour and a love of teasing. And they were both terrible flirts.

Contemporaries were convinced that they had fallen in love and that was clearly the view of Elizabeth's family. 'He was an absolute heart-throb and they fell for each other in a big way. It was obvious when you saw them together that they were madly in love,' says Elizabeth's dresser, Mabel Monty. According to one elderly courtier and to one of Elizabeth's close relations, 'He was the love of her life.'

Although there is no record of any formal engagement, James almost certainly proposed to her in private. In those days a young man could scarcely even kiss a young lady without making it plain that his intentions were strictly honourable. Whatever the truth of the matter, it is clear that Elizabeth did not instantly succumb. She was young and headstrong but not frivolous or likely to act without serious con-sideration. If James harried, she hesitated.

'My father was drop down-dead handsome,' says James's daughter. 'He never had to make the slightest effort; women just fell at his feet. He had a take-it-or-leave-it attitude and they couldn't resist it. All he had to do was raise an eyebrow or give them a half smile and they were captivated. I have never known a man like him with women.'

He was well-born, a war hero, witty and handsome. Thus, for any of the young women in Elizabeth's circle, he was a considerable catch. Should she reel him in?

CHAPTER EIGHT

Elizabeth's dilemma

· · · ◁━◆━▷ · · ·

E ARLY IN 1920, Elizabeth's parents reluctantly had to leave 20 St James's Square when the lease ended, and after much difficulty moved to 17 Bruton Street. The new house needed a great deal of work, so for the season that year Elizabeth stayed with her sister Rosie.

By May, James was back in London to take up his royal appointment, and was installed on the same floor as the schoolroom at Buckingham Palace. A great many perks came with the job and it was 'an interesting experience', yet he remembers that it was 'a somewhat lonely life'. He would often retreat to the Prince of Wales's somewhat livelier quarters for a little light relief. Here he could join his childhood friends Claud Hamilton, Godfrey Thomas and Bruce Ogilvy, who belonged to the prince's inner circle of cronies. Prince George, later the Duke of Kent, also sought sanctuary at his elder brother's place when he came home on leave from the Navy. 'He found more freedom there to come and go as he wished, and I certainly didn't blame him,' James recalled.

Although James was later to describe Prince Albert as 'not an easy man to know or handle', he was aware of the sort of childhood the future King had experienced and was sympathetic. Of Bertie's father, King George V, James observed:

> In his relations with his children there remained something of the manner of a stern and caustic naval commander ... Certainly he had clear-cut views and he expressed them – with his wishes and criticisms – in no uncertain terms. He was well versed in the language of the gun-room and the ward-room, but the idea of dealing with children by such methods as discussion and persuasion was foreign to him, which I think was a pity.

The strictness of the royal household is illustrated in a story James tells about a proposed tennis party. Princess Mary apparently could

A tennis party at the Strathmores. James is standing behind Elizabeth, with Bertie on her left

150

not play because she had to have tea with the King and Queen and could not possibly wear her tennis shoes because the King would take a poor view of such behaviour. 'I mention this only to give some idea of the strict code of behaviour upon which George V insisted even within the family. The case of the princess's shoes also recalls the occasion when the King first saw the Prince of Wales wearing trousers with turned-up bottoms and asked coldly if it was muddy outside.'

Yet as the season progressed James's life was far from dull. Elizabeth was close at hand, his mantelpiece was four-deep in invitations and he enjoyed all the cachet of a royal position. The season rolled on and the young royal equerry was in the thick of it.

Some found the relentless round of fun overwhelming. Prince Paul of Serbia wrote to his friend Jean, Comte de Ribes in July 1920 from St Paul's Walden Bury:

> I have meant to write to you a million times before but every time I sat down to do so, I was caught up in the maelstrom of the London season. Never has the London season been more brilliant and I am so sorry that you were not part of it.
>
> The reason I have fled and am resting at the Strathmores is the fatiguing nature of the week before. There were masses of balls: Lady Violet Astor, Ribblesdale, Vandenlenen and lastly Portland. The last one was much the best although small (100 people). Everyone wore 'breeches' which was very pretty. The tables were covered in Queen Anne linen.

In addition to the formal entertainments, the debutantes of the day were only too ready to take part in any prank or escapade. Lady Rachel gives a lively account of breaking into her old home, Devonshire House, which had been sold and was then let out for receptions and dances. The raiding party included her sister Dorothy, her brother-in-law Harold Macmillan and Harry Cator.

> We climbed up to the roof where there was a glass dome and managed to open one of the windows from where we had a wonderful view of all the guests arriving and walking up the wide marble staircase. One of our party, Harry Cator, had had the forethought to bring an awful-looking spider with long legs made of wire springs, which we attached to a reel of black cotton and dangled in front of the guests as they walked up the stairs.
>
> The spider was about the size of a golf ball without the legs and the smart people below were horrified. Luckily nobody came onto the roof to turn us off but we thought it best to remove ourselves before there was any trouble and made our way onto the floor of the house where all our bedrooms used to be.

152

We did not think there would be anyone up there but we were wrong. It was a very wet night and we were all in mackintoshes looking awful. We wandered about looking at all our old rooms and Harold Macmillan, for some reason I don't know why, went into what used to be the nursery pantry where he found a young couple playing snuggle puppy, who were very surprised to see a dripping figure in the doorway. They asked him what he wanted and he said 'A tin opener' which was as good an answer as any other!

The other participants in the adventure remain anonymous. But Elizabeth was a close friend of Rachel Cavendish and never slow to join in a little innocent mischief. James too was always ready for any excitement.

They were both at a ball given by Lord and Lady Farquhar early in the season, where they spent much of the evening fox-trotting together. Prince Albert was also among the guests and, according to James, asked to be introduced to his pretty dancing partner. James is not a very reliable witness, but he was correct on this occasion. The prince was later to claim that he had fallen in love with Elizabeth that night, although he did not realise it until later.

James was still engaged to Elfie but he and Elizabeth were constant companions. Lady Elizabeth's dresser recalls the *billets doux* that would be secretly exchanged via the good offices of housemaids. Her niece, the Hon. Jean Wills, remembers that her aunt told her of an occasion in London when Elizabeth had broken all the rules and slipped out unnoticed to lunch with a young man. Just who he was she never confessed. But James could be very persuasive.

During the winter of 1920-21 Queen Mary and her Mistress of the Robes, the Duchess of Devonshire, were considering the advantages of a marriage between Her Grace's fourth daughter and Prince Bertie. Rachel Cavendish was a sweet-natured girl and an entirely suitable wife for the King's younger son.

Lady Rachel was asked to stay at Windsor Castle for the Ascot race meeting and put in a room next to Princess Mary, with a shared sitting-room. 'The princes came to our sitting-room sometimes,' she recalled:

The Prince of Wales had stayed with us in Canada so I knew him and the others were very easy and ready to get away from the somewhat sticky atmosphere of the whole place. They were all very kind to me. Having been brought up at Government House, I knew how to behave as my father represented the King there. It may seem silly now, but we always had to curtsey to him as we left the room and little things like that, so I was well trained and not in the least nervous about anything.

The Mad Hatters and their admirers. Standing from left: Lord Gage, James Stuart and Prince Paul. Sitting with Elizabeth and her mother are, left to right: Katharine Hamilton, Grisell Cochrane-Baillie, Miss Blackburn and Diamond Hardinge. The keen photographer on Elizabeth's left is identified only as Francis

154

One evening when the Prince of Wales came to our sitting-room, he was busily chewing gum, a habit he had acquired in Canada, to the horror of a great many people. This particular evening, he gave me a bit, which I also enjoyed. When the time came to go down to dinner, I had to get rid of it and stuck it behind a mirror.

By now Bertie was aware that he was smitten with Elizabeth Bowes Lyon. He began taking every opportunity to see her, both at St Paul's and Glamis. His path was reluctantly smoothed by none other than his equerry, James, who could hardly refuse when his master expressed a wish to come along too.

Outwardly, James's relationship with Elizabeth appeared to be closer than ever. Elfie, who had failed to provide the right sort of solace to James's war-damaged spirits, was no longer involved. Elizabeth had both soothed and cheered him. On her part, his courtship was wonderfully exciting. But it had also given her a great deal to think about. As an intelligent young woman she could not fail to see the dangers or recognise that, captivating as James was, he was all too easily attracted to young women. Michael, who was so fond of her and who knew James well, may also have put her on her guard.

Bill Deedes, the former Tory politician and editor of the *Daily Telegraph*, served in the cabinet with James. He remembers his old colleague vividly:

> James was a deeply attractive chap. He was laid-back to the point of insolence and yet he had a cutting edge. As Churchill's Chief Whip, if a young MP stepped out of line, he would snap and they would never forget it. His air was deceptive. He had bite.
>
> I can imagine any girl falling for him but I suspect she wouldn't neccesarily have seen him as a future husband. She would have said to herself: this is a lovely man to be seen out with. Lots of girls are like that. They don't neccesarily intend marriage seriously but they are happy to be seen in his company. You could make all the other girls envious.
>
> James was the sort of man that if you went to a dance with him on your arm, you could be totally confident that no girl could do any better. Girls like to feel proud of the chap they are going out with. That's very important to a girl.

'Pretty women flocked round him and he loved every minute of it,' says James's daughter, echoing Lord Deedes. 'He couldn't resist it and I think Elizabeth slowly came to realise that he was, perhaps, not husband material.' There were other considerations: 'While they obviously had a huge affection for each other, neither of them had a bean and he had no prospects. They both needed to marry money.'

Queen Mary, meanwhile, was left in no doubt by Prince Bertie of the virtues of Lady Elizabeth and had taken her beady eye off Lady Rachel Cavendish as a prospective daughter-in-law. Her Majesty decided to go herself to visit the Strathmores' Scottish castle.

In view of certain events that had occurred during her recent visit there, it is significant that The Queen was prepared to travel up to Glamis to consider the marriage prospects of one of her children.

On the previous occasion, too, Lady Elizabeth had been involved, though not directly. In addition to The Queen, the house-party had included her daughter Princess Mary and Lord Dalkeith, son of the seventh Duke of Buccleuch. Queen Mary had already laid plans for her daughter's marriage, and was unaware that Lord Dalkeith and the princess were deeply in love. The illicit attachment was known only to a few of the princess's most trusted friends, one of whom was Elizabeth.

The two young women had met through their mutual work for the Girl Guide Movement – Lady Elizabeth was District Commissioner for Glamis and Eassie Parish – and they were soon on the best of terms. It was through the princess that Lady Elizabeth was first invited to Buckingham Palace.

The Strathmores' royal guests duly arrived. Mabel Monty takes up the previously untold story:

> The princess was madly in love with Lord Dalkeith, the Duke of Buccleuch's son, and he with her. However it had to be kept the deepest, darkest secret because it was known that Queen Mary would not approve.
>
> Although he was heir to one of the most ancient dukedoms in the country and an extremely nice young man, it was thought in some circles that he was not rich enough to marry the King's only daughter. In those days parents were accustomed, and indeed expected, to ensure the most advantageous match possible for their offspring, and the Queen was no exception. Henry Lascelles was already being considered as a possible bridegroom and the Queen would brook no interference with her carefully laid plans. So everyone kept mum and waited to see what would happen.
>
> When the princess was staying at Glamis, she was given Lady Strathmore's private sitting-room, known as the Tapestry Room, for her own personal use. It was there that she and Lord Dalkeith could meet à deux, well away from her mother's and Lady Strathmore's eagle eyes.
>
> The way they managed it was most ingenious and required careful planning and perfect timing. They also had to rely on the discretion of a handful of the most trusted servants, whom they hoped would not betray them.
>
> The conspiracy worked this way. The pair of them would retire to their rooms on some pretext, well before the dressing bell, was sounded and

A visit by the Princess Royal
to Chatsworth in 1921.
Princess Mary is in the front
row, third from the left. James
Stuart is third from the left in
the back row and Rachel
Cavendish is on the far right,
back row

get themselves ready for dinner. Then a little while after the bell was sounded, when everyone else was safely out of the way in their rooms, having baths and putting on their evening dress, and lookouts had been posted at strategic points, a footman would lead Lord Dalkeith down back staircases and little used corridors to the Tapestry Room. Once there the door was quietly closed and the lovebirds could enjoy a brief spell together.

The plan worked well for some time, but an unguarded glance or an indiscreet gesture may have given the pair away, or one of the servants may have hoped to curry favour by revealing the princess's secret. At all events, Queen Mary became suspicious of the romance and determined to catch the pair red-handed.

The day progressed as usual. The princess made her excuses after tea and retired to her room. Lord Dalkeith also left and made his way to the private sitting-room. Moments later, to the horror of the lookouts, the Queen came sweeping round the corner and, before there was time to raise the alarm, burst through the door of the Tapestry Room to find her daughter in the arms of Lord Dalkeith.

'I have never heard a row like it,' remembers Miss Monty:

> The Queen was beside herself with fury and the shouting could be heard all over the castle. Lord Dalkeith was immediately chucked out of the house and told his possessions would be sent on. Princess Mary never appeared at dinner. It was said she had a bad headache but of course everyone knew otherwise.
>
> We all thought it very sad because they were such a sweet young couple and it was all so romantic. What the Strathmore family thought of it all, I have no idea, but it must have been rather embarrassing.
>
> I was a good friend of Princess Mary's dresser, Miss Green, and she told me that the night before her wedding, the princess lay in her arms and cried her heart out. The trouble was that the Buccleuchs may have been rich but the Lascelleses were worth millions.

Undaunted by this memory, Queen Mary made her visit to Glamis to inspect Elizabeth Bowes Lyon. It confirmed her growing conviction that Elizabeth might indeed be a suitable bride for Bertie.

Lady Strathmore, with a royal suitor in the wings, was also having second thoughts about her daughter's future. Perhaps James Stuart no longer seemed suitable, particularly in view of his behaviour and reputation. With admirable directness, she decided to involve James's mother, Lady Moray, in the deliberations.

'In the end everybody put their heads together and it was decided that it would be best if my father went away for a while,' says James's son, Viscount Stuart of Findhorn. 'And so he was dispatched to the

In the first days of 1922 James
was banished to Oklahoma –
and his rival's way was clear.
This is the photo he sent
home to Elizabeth, which she
kept in her private collection
ever after

James, left, on an oil-rig in
Oklahoma later in the same
year. In his autobiography he
confessed 'I was frightened to
death'

oil fields of Oklahoma to be a rigger. By the time he came home, Lady Elizabeth was not only engaged but married to the Duke of York.'

At Glamis that New Year, 1922, there was only one visitor – James Stuart. Perhaps this was when he and Lady Elizabeth said their goodbyes. A few days later, he left for America.

'I will always remember my father saying that there was no point in marrying for love because love does not last but money does,' says James's daughter. 'I have always understood that my mother and father's engagement was drawn up by a solicitor. It was arranged. She had the money and he had the name.'

James's wife was 'just the sort of woman he wanted,' according to the perceptive Cynthia Munro, daughter of Elfie. 'She was beautiful, she was rich, she was the most marvellously loyal and tolerant kind of wife that any philanderer could have hoped to have.' The woman she was describing was Rachel Cavendish.

The engagement of James Stuart and Lady Rachel Cavendish was announced in *The Times* on 25 April 1923, the day before Elizabeth's wedding day. They were married in the village church on the Devonshire family's Chatsworth estate, on 4 August 1923. It was Elizabeth's twenty-third birthday.

Rachel Cavendish's loyalty and tolerance were never more tested than on the occasion of a notorious divorce scandal in the late 1940s involving a certain Mrs Archer Clive, her husband the brigadier and the Hon. James Stuart.

James and Mrs Archer Clive, who was the daughter of Lord Portman, had met in Arizona where he was recovering from a sinus operation after ill health had forced him to resign from the cabinet. She was a great society beauty, just the sort of sophisticated woman who pleased him best. What is more, her husband was nowhere in sight and James, for once, had time on his hands.

They were staying with old friends, Herbert and Barbie Agar, who were determined that their guests should have a good time. James was at his sparkling best. Over cocktails and candlelit dinners, he set out to charm his companion. She, flattered but coy, initially resisted his advances but soon it became apparent that once again James would succeed.

Quite what he promised the beautiful thirty-five-year-old was later to tax the brains of some of the most eminent lawyers in the land. In any event, a passionate affair ensued. When the time came to go home the lovers said their farewells, promising to meet in Britain. And that was that, thought James. However, for once, it was not going to be that easy. Penelope Isobel was a tenacious mistress. She made no

James and Rachel Cavendish
marry at the Duke of
Devonshire's home,
Chatsworth House, on
4 August 1923 –
Elizabeth's 23rd birthday

secret of her infatuation and confessed the liaison to her husband, who decided to divorce her. A scandal loomed and it looked as if Churchill's former Chief Whip would be named as co-respondent.

Moreover, Mrs Archer Clive fully expected him to do the decent thing when the court proceedings were over. James fumed and fretted, pacing round the drawing-room of Landford Lodge, his country home in the New Forest. 'He was in stinking mood, crashing and banging about the place,' remembers his daughter Davina Ritchie. 'Nothing could be done to please him. He was filled with a deep anger.'

Finally, in desperation, he confessed all to his long-suffering wife, Lady Rachel. 'My mother asked him if he actually wanted to marry this woman to which he replied, "Of course not!" says Mrs Ritchie. 'To him it had just been a pleasant flirtation and he was perfectly happy with the way things were. The last thing he wanted to do was to break up the marriage.'

Lady Rachel offered to try to resolve the situation and James, much relieved, readily agreed. 'My mother put on her smartest dress and best hat and set off for the station. There she bought a cheap day return to London and boarded the train. A taxi took her directly to the woman's flat and she swept in to tell her the bad news. She made it quite plain that, despite their previous liaison, her husband had no intention of marrying her and would consider it a great favour if he was kept out of her divorce.' However, Lady Rachel's intervention was to no avail and James was duly cited in the court proceedings.

James had had affairs with just about every society beauty who would have him, most notably with the Duchess of Buccleuch, nicknamed Midnight Moll because she was so often to be found prowling corridors late at night. But this time the game was really up. As his sister Hermione commented wryly at the time, 'Poor old James has been caught out at last.' It was just before his fifty-second birthday.

There is a sad and intriguing footnote to the story. In 1971, James telephoned The Queen Mother and asked to see her. She invited him for lunch. Two days later, James died. As his daughter confirms, 'Even now Queen Elizabeth's face will light up at the mention of his name. They may both have married somebody else, but they always remained close friends.'

Rachel Cavendish. 'The most tolerant wife any philanderer could hope for'

CHAPTER NINE

A modest proposal

· · · ⟨⟨⟨◈⟩⟩⟩ · · ·

LIKE HIS FATHER, Bertie was the second son. George V had become the heir to the throne on the early death of his elder brother whose fiancée, Princess Mary of Teck, he then married. Also like his father, until he became king Bertie held the title Duke of York. There the similarity ends for King George was a dour figure, both as a monarch and as a parent. Yet, in his awkward way, he was affectionate towards his children and particularly towards his own second son. 'Bertie,' he used to say, 'has more guts than the rest of them put together.' It was a shrewd comment, especially coming from a father whose gruffness and insensitivity threatened to scar the young prince's character for life. Bertie had been an ailing, difficult child, retreating into moody silences whenever he was forced to undertake a disagreeable task. The victim of a brutish nurse, a disciplinarian tutor and his parents' apparent indifference, he had neither the charm nor the boldness of his older brother David. Yet in spite of his shy, stammering manner, Bertie grew into a man of dogged determination. This quality, together with his gentle and considerate nature, eventually won him the hand of Lady Elizabeth Bowes Lyon.

Nevertheless, it was a struggle. He was the King's son, wealthy and good-looking, but in other respects he was an unprepossessing wooer. In those early years of peace, he lacked the glamour of distinguished war service. Bertie had seen action briefly aboard HMS *Collingwood* in the battle of Jutland, from which both he and the ship emerged unscathed. Otherwise the most dangerous moments of his naval career occurred in ships' sick bays or in hospitals ashore, when he was suffering from appendicitis, ulcers and soused-mackerel poisoning.

His royal status gave him little advantage; if anything, it proved a handicap. The Bowes Lyon family had no tradition as courtiers and

Elizabeth and Bertie at Glamis in 1921

had even developed an aversion to the court, although Mabell, Lady Airlie, one of Lady Strathmore's closest friends, was a lady-in-waiting to Queen Mary. Lord Strathmore, a devout and decent man, thoroughly disapproved of the amorous adventures of the Prince of Wales, later King Edward VIII, and swore that 'if there is one thing I have determined for my children, it is that they shall never have any post about the court.' In the circumstances, persistence was Bertie's only hope.

Lord Strathmore himself was partly to blame for the belief that Prince Bertie and Lady Elizabeth were childhood friends as, 'laughing happily', he described them to the world's press after the engagement was announced. They may have encountered each other as children, given the circles in which they both moved. There is one particular story which relates how, at a birthday party given by Lady Leicester, the ten-year-old Bertie is said to have been deeply impressed when Elizabeth, aged five, gave him the cherries from the top of her cake.

It is certainly true that Elizabeth was later introduced to the royal family by Bertie's sister, Princess Mary. As we have seen, they shared an interest in the Girl Guides and became friends when Elizabeth was District Commissioner for Glamis and Eassie Parish and the princess reviewed the troop while staying with Lady Airlie at nearby Cortachy Castle. In London the two girls liked to dance to the princess's gramophone records in her apartment at Buckingham Palace. Inevitably her brothers would drop in and Bertie may have met Elizabeth there.

It is typical of James Stuart's sometime inaccurate memoirs, however, that he claims the credit for introducing the future King and Queen. Unfortunately, he gets both the year wrong (1921 instead of 1920), and also the occasion. In his autobiography, he writes:

> In the summer of 1921 the first Royal Air Force Ball was held at the Ritz Hotel and my master, the Duke of York, was guest of honour, having joined the RAF from the Navy during the war. He gave a small dinner party at the Berkeley and then we walked across to the Ritz. I was on duty, so I saw the party settled in, and then sought out my own friends. Later in the evening HRH came over to me and asked who was the girl with whom I had just been dancing. I told him that her name was Elizabeth Bowes Lyon and he asked if I would introduce him, which I did.
>
> It was a more significant moment than it was possible then to realise but it is certainly true to say that from then on he never showed the slightest interest in any other young lady.

Had such an introduction been necessary, it would appear to have taken place in 1920 at a ball given on 20 May by Lord and Lady

Farquhar at 7 Grosvenor Square. In other respects, the story is much as in James's version. Bertie is said to have told his mother's faithful lady-in-waiting, Lady Airlie, that he had fallen in love that evening although he did not realise it until later.

Whatever the truth of the encounter, it is clear that from this time Bertie was convinced that he had found the woman he wanted to marry. He pursued her single-mindedly for the next thirty-two months.

Bertie was seeking companionship as well as love. According to James Stuart, he presented a somewhat solitary figure in post-war London, when most of the young people in his milieu seemed to be enjoying one long round of entertainment. He had no close friends of his own age. This would have pleased his great-grandmother, Queen Victoria, who instructed all her children that while it was right and civil to be friendly towards those one might occasionally meet outside the charmed circle, it was extremely unwise to make 'friendships' as 'intimacies are very bad & often lead to great mischief'. The best course of action was to stick to one's own relations – 'you want no one *else*,' she added.

During his childhood years, Bertie did not have anybody else, apart from his siblings. David, Bertie and their younger sister Mary all suffered at the hands of a 'sadistic and incompetent' nurse who, as the Duke of Windsor later wrote, reduced all three children to 'sobbing and bawling'. According to Lady Mary Clayton:

> When Albert was a baby she often gave him his afternoon bottle while driving in a carriage notorious for its swaying motion, which produced an effect not unlike sea sickness. The child was always sick and, thanks to this treatment in early life, went on to develop chronic stomach problems which led to the gastric trouble he was to suffer as a young man. She was a very fierce, unpleasant nanny who mistreated them all – but Bertie suffered the most.

By the time the Duchess of York (as Queen Mary then was) discovered the nurse's true character, they were suffering from rickets, a disease normally associated with the half-starved inhabitants of the slums. Perhaps this explains Bertie's later problems with his knock knees.

Lady Mary Clayton continues, 'It was only through the courage of the nursery footman that the Duke and Duchess ever found out what was going on. He was horrified by the nursery regime and finally decided something had to be done. So he handed in his notice and told the duke.'

Mabel Monty remembers the stories her mother-in-law, Christina Stringer, used to tell her about the nurse's reign at York House. Mrs Stringer was the maternity nurse at Sandringham and had been present at the birth of all the royal babies.

> She told me that the nurse was so harsh and so strict that the children had a worse life than any of the village youngsters. She used to hit them with a big rod for no reason and never cared for them at all. They weren't even properly fed.
>
> She was particularly cruel to Prince Albert because he had a stutter and had temper tantrums; but the more she hit him with the rod, the more difficult he became. She was dreadful to him. According to my mother-in-law when she vented her anger on him with the rod, he would just cower away and hide. She had a long reign but the footman finally put paid to her.

She was replaced by the under-nurse, nicknamed Lala, who seems to have been more kindly.

The Duke and Duchess of York saw relatively little of their children until they were in their teens. 'If any of them were ill, their parents never went to see them,' says Mabel Monty. 'They wouldn't have dreamt of going into the same room in case they caught something. The duchess was very distant.'

In fact, the duke and duchess were the most anxious of parents but, like so many upper-class parents of their generation, they had no notion of how to bring up children. They spent hours agonising over their education and futures but little time actually with them. The duke was by nature a martinet and his pride in his family made him over-quick to find fault. He was tidy, punctual, hard-working and a stickler for tradition. On Bertie's fifth birthday, he received a letter from his father which read: 'Now that you are five years old, I hope you will always try to be obedient & do at once what you are told, as you will find it will come much easier to you the sooner you begin. I always tried to do this when I was your age & found it made me much happier.' There was no other greeting.

The young princes' lives improved when they were put in the charge of Frederick Finch, a friendly nursery footman. From then on he tended to all needs, from hearing their prayers to shining their shoes. Another, less welcome innovation, came early one spring morning in 1902, as the Duke of Windsor later recalled:

> Bertie and I heard my father stamping up the stairs. He had a particularly heavy footfall, but on that particular morning it sounded more ominous than ever. Besides, it was not his habit to come often to our room. In

some apprehension we watched the door. When it opened, it revealed next to my father a tall, gaunt, solemn stranger with a large moustache. 'This is Mr Hansell,' my father said coldly, 'your new tutor.' And with that he walked out of the room, leaving us alone with Mr Hansell, who was no doubt as embarrassed as we were.

Mr Hansell, or 'Mider' as he was christened, immediately set about correcting Bertie's left-handedness, and in so doing almost certainly aggravated his stammer. Mider quickly discovered that the young prince was hopeless at mathematics, an essential subject if he were to be accepted into the Royal Naval College, Osborne, as his father wished. In one gloomy report, Mr Hansell noted: 'The work in simple division sums is most disheartening. I really thought we had mastered division by 3 but division by 2 seems to be quite beyond him now.' Bertie was by then nearly six years old.

Despite such stories, Bertie was not stupid, merely nervous and shy. He was a particular favourite of his mother's lady-in-waiting, Lady Airlie, who recalls this telling incident in her book, *Thatched with Gold*:

> He made his first shy overture to me at Easter 1902 ... when he presented me with an Easter card. It was his own work, and very well done for a child of six – a design of spring flowers and chicks, evidently cut out of a magazine, coloured in crayons, and pasted on cardboard. He was so anxious for me to receive it in time for Easter that he decided to deliver it in person. He waylaid me one morning when I came out of his mother's boudoir, but at the last moment his courage failed him, and thrusting the card in my hand without a word he darted away.
>
> When I succeeded later in gaining his confidence, he talked to me quite normally, without stammering, and then I found that far from being backward, he was an intelligent child, with more force of character than anyone expected in those days.

Bertie seldom encountered such a sympathetic listener. Struggling with his schoolwork and his stammer made him moody and frustrated. To add to his misery, the royal doctor recommended a drastic cure for his knock knees: he was to wear splints for several hours every day and during the night. 'This is an experiment,' the eight-year-old wrote to his mother. 'I am sitting in an armchair with my legs in the new splints ... I have got an invalid table, which is splendid for reading but rather awkward for writing at present ... I expect I shall get used to it,' he adds plaintively. The remedy did work, however, and Bertie grew up with perfectly straight legs.

The boys' favourite teacher was the local village schoolmaster, Walter Jones, who stood in when Mider was away on holiday. A keen naturalist, he took Bertie on long walks through the woods and marshes of Sandringham, instilling in him a lasting love of birdlife and the countryside. Bertie was also a natural athlete who would one day play tennis at Wimbledon and for the RAF. He also became an excellent horseman: the pages of the *Tatler* magazine after the First World War regularly carried reports of his riding with various hunts. When the lakes froze over Bertie and David would make up ice-hockey teams with boys from the Sandringham estate to play local sides. Mr Jones also organised football teams made up of the princes and boys from the school at West Newton. They would then take on local sides with David as captain. Mabel Monty's future husband Alfred Stringer, whose family had been tenant farmers on the Sandringham estate since the time of Queen Victoria, was one of the boys picked for the royal team.

> My husband was the same age as Prince Albert and he used to tell me how a tutor and a footman would bring the princes down from York Cottage for matches. They would play cricket or rounders or football depending on the season.
>
> He said the tutor kept a strict eye on the game which he very much controlled – not too much rough and tumble was encouraged. There was quite of lot of 'don't do this' and 'don't do that' but they managed to enjoy themselves nonetheless.
>
> It was about the only time that the royal children were allowed to mix with youngsters of their own age. They were not encouraged to have friends but to rely on each other for company. My husband said that Prince Albert was very shy but a nice fellow and good footballer. In later years when they met at tenants' parties or fêtes he always came up to speak to him.

Relying on other members of his family for company was small comfort when Bertie was sent to Osborne in 1909, shortly after his fourteenth birthday. It was his first time away from home and among boys of his own age. He found life hard and lonely and his stammer made matters worse. His older brother was unable to help, as strict rules forbade senior boys to mix with younger ones. Within six months, Bertie had contracted whooping cough and was ordered home to convalesce by the young surgeon-lieutenant, Louis Greig, who was to have a profound impact on his adult life. This was the first of many bouts of ill-health he was to suffer over the succeeding years.

Bertie was placed near the bottom of his class, but in spite of this, two years later he passed into Dartmouth Naval College and again joined his brother. A month after his arrival, an epidemic of mumps and measles broke out from which two cadets died. Bertie and David

The Prince of Wales,
the Duke of York and
the Duke of Gloucester

were moved into the commandant's house to escape infection, yet caught both diseases and their condition was sufficiently severe to warrant bulletins being published in the *Lancet*.

By this time, the princes' father had acceded to the throne and on 22 June 1911 been crowned King George V. Prince Albert's altered status led to some embarrassment when in 1913 he undertook a six-month training cruise to qualify as a midshipman. At every port of call, the hospitality on shore was agonising for the shy cadet: every girl wanted to dance with the King's son and he was terrified at the prospect.

Ill-heath plagued Bertie throughout the First World War. Three weeks after the declaration of hostilities he was rushed into the port of Aberdeen to have his appendix removed. After three months' convalescence, he again experienced acute stomach pains and was given a job at the Admiralty. However, it proved to be a sinecure and he had nothing to do. His pleas to be sent back to his ship, HMS *Collingwood*, were finally granted, but within three months he was back on the hospital ship and declared unfit for active service. It was a terrible blow for Bertie as it was for his father, who overruled the physician's advice: 'The King would prefer to run the risk of Prince Albert's health suffering than that he should endure the bitter and lasting disappointment of not being in his ship in the battle line.' However, it was not until the end of May 1916 that Bertie was fit to return to HMS *Collingwood*. The battle of Jutland was about to begin and here at last was his moment of glory. He later gave his own account of it:

> I was in a turret and watched most of the action through one of the trainer's telescopes as we were firing by Director, when the turret is trained in the working chamber and not in the gun house. At the commencement I was sitting on top of a turret and had a very good view of the proceedings. I was up there during a lull, when a German ship started firing at us, and one salvo 'straddled' us. We at once returned fire. I was distinctly startled and jumped down the hole in the top of the turret like a shot rabbit!! I didn't try the experience again …
>
> The hands behaved splendidly and all of them in the best spirits as their heart's desire had at last been granted, which was to be in action with the Germans. Some of the turret's crew actually took on bets with one another that we should not fire a shot. A good deal of money must have changed hands I should think by now.
>
> My impressions were very different from what I expected. I saw visions of the masts going over the side and funnels hurtling through the air etc. In reality none of these things happened and we are still quite as sound as we were before. No one would know to look at the ship that she had been in action. It was certainly a great experience to have been through and it shows that we are at war and that the Germans can fight if they like.

He wrote to his brother David: 'When I was on top of the turret, I never felt any fear of shells or anything else. It seems curious but all sense of danger and everything else goes except the one longing to deal death in every possible way to the enemy.'

'In a single summer afternoon, he passed into the full dignity of manhood,' wrote his official biographer, Sir John Wheeler-Bennett. But despite this show of fighting spirit, Bertie was to be denied further involvement in the war. Three months after the battle, he was back at Windsor Castle where a duodenal ulcer was diagnosed and he was again prescribed rest – nine months this time. He finally managed to rejoin his ship in the following May but within three months he was home again, unfit for duty. His old friend from Osborne, Surgeon-Lieutenant Louis Greig, returned with him and urged him to inform his father that he was not fit enough for service at sea. During four years at war, he had only been able to serve his country for twenty-two months.

A successful operation was performed on his ulcer in November 1917 and by the beginning of the following year Bertie, accompanied by Louis Greig, whom he described as a 'perfect topper', was transferred to the Royal Naval Air Service and posted to General Trenchard's headquarters in France. Bertie was desperate to see more action but within two weeks of their arrival the Armistice was declared and the war was over.

Nothing had so far gone well for Prince Bertie. An anxious childhood, solitary schooldays, regular illness and a disappointing war had done nothing to build up his self-confidence. A spell up at Cambridge, where he met virtually no one outside his own family, can only have deepened his despondency, even though his father bestowed on him 'that fine old title of Duke of York' while he was there. By the time he left Cambridge in 1920 and returned to London, he was prone to bouts of moroseness accompanied by heavy whisky-drinking. He still had no male friends, apart from his brother and Louis Greig, fifteen years his senior, let alone any female ones.

At that time, when wealthy, well-connected young men openly pursued the glamorous actresses and music-hall stars of the day, it is hardly surprising that Bertie had an encounter with Phyllis Monkman, an actress and dancer who had appeared on stage since the age of twelve.

Three years older than Bertie and no great beauty, she had laughing eyes, a vibrant personality and sensational legs. She had played with Jack Hulbert and counted Noel Coward and Ivor Novello among her intimate friends. In 1919, when she was starring with Jack Buchanan in the hit show *Tails Up* at the Comedy Theatre, Louis Greig suddenly appeared at her dressing-room door one night and told her that Prince Albert wanted to meet her and take her out to dinner. She met Bertie, very discreetly, at a house in Half Moon Street.

According to his biographer Sarah Bradford:

> More than that she would not say and no more is known of the romance, beyond rumours in the social-theatrical world of annual presents of jewellery on her birthday and the fact that among her effects when she died, aged eighty-four, on 2 December 1976, was a small scuffed leather wallet with a flap purpose-made to hold one photograph and stiff enough to stand on its own like a miniature frame. Inside it was a portrait of Prince Albert in a dark blue peaked cap with wings, soft shirt collar pinned behind a dark blue tie, the lapels of his Service greatcoat just visible.

Prince Albert also showed an interest in Lord Londonderry's beautiful and assertive daughter, Lady Maureen Vane-Tempest-Stewart, whose parents were close friends of the royal family. Lady Londonderry was surrounded by a charmed circle of acquaintances and so was universally known as Circe. She was one of the great hostesses of the day and a patroness of writers, including George Bernard Shaw and W. B. Yeats.

She gave a weekly dance for her children to which, as family friends, Bertie and his brothers were invited and it was at one of these that Bertie first met Lady Maureen. The interest was obviously mutual and Lady Londonderry told Harold Nicolson that her daughter might have been Queen of England. However, Maureen preferred Lord Derby's younger son Oliver Stanley, and became engaged to him in the summer of 1920.

By that time, as we know, Bertie had already turned his attention to Lady Elizabeth Bowes Lyon and through the good (if reluctant) offices of his equerry, had procured a weekend invitation to St Paul's Walden Bury. The prince was captivated not only by Elizabeth but by the relaxed atmosphere that prevailed there. Guests were allowed to do much as they liked, playing games, drinking cocktails and lounging in the sunny gardens – a marked contrast to the formality of his parents' cheerless household.

The prince already knew Lady Elizabeth's brother Michael, who was a contemporary of his older brother David, and the other visitors were all familiar from the London social scene. In this friendly environment, Bertie forgot his self-conciousness and joined in with the rest of the party. Tennis was a favourite occupation at St Paul's and, an excellent player, he had an opportunity to shine.

Photographs of Bertie at the various Strathmore homes show him looking handsome and at ease. According to Lady Mary Clayton, he was a very attractive man:

> He was tall and fair and good looking. Although David had the charisma, many people preferred his younger brother because he was so kind and gentle. He was wonderful at games, there was nothing he wasn't good at. He was a marvellous tennis player but he was also good at cricket and croquet and could be a very determined competitor.
>
> In private his stutter was, if anything, quite attractive – the slight hesitation adding to his charm. He was quite unlike his other brothers in that he was very artistic. He was such a keen observer and never missed the slightest detail. He would have made a wonderful painter.
>
> He had a rather rude sense of humour. As children, we all thought him very funny. I remember bumping into him and the Prince of Wales when they were staying at Glamis. We had just been at the dressing-up box and were coming down a very narrow passage. He introduced us to his brother. We were very embarrassed because we were so squashed up that it was impossible to curtsey properly. He just laughed and thought it very amusing.

One aspect of the prince's character that must have appealed to Elizabeth was his strong sense of purpose. After the war he threw himself into a strenuous round of royal duties. His stammer could sometimes be a problem yet in July 1920 he made an impressive speech at the Royal Agricultural Show in Darlington, concluding with conviction: 'Land must go back to the plough, for grass will not support us.'

Despite the reservations of some of the King's advisers, he became the first president of the Boys' Welfare Association. This was a progressive organisation which aimed to improve the lot of young men working in industry. Its scope was soon extended to cover the relationship between employers and working men of all ages, urging the need for such amenities as canteen facilities and medical care.

The strong sense of commitment with which the prince visited factories, mines and shipyards led his brothers to nickname him 'the

Doing the social round. Bertie shying – left-handed – during the Fresh Air Fund outing, Loughton

A Glamis house-party in 1921.
Back row: Bertie is second
from the left, James third
from the right. Elizabeth is
seated beween Arthur Penn
and Katharine Hamilton

Elizabeth sitting between
Bertie and Arthur Penn,
another of her famous hats at
her feet

Bertie on the moors at
Glamis. He was ashamed of
his poor marksmanship, and
took special lessons to
improve his technique

Another tennis party at
Glamis. Elizabeth and Bertie
loved the game. On the left
are Helen Cecil and
Katharine Hamilton

Foreman'; yet his hard work was recognised by the unions. One trade unionist wrote: 'At no time in the history of this or any other country has anyone, occupying a similar position to the Duke of York, done so much to establish and maintain harmonious relationships between employers and workmen ... [he] has placed the community under an obligation to him for the kindliness and effectiveness with which he has performed the tasks allotted to him.'

Bertie's strong social conscience no doubt won the approval of Elizabeth. The Strathmore children had been brought up to help those less fortunate than themselves, visiting the sick on the Glamis estate and supporting local charities. Elizabeth's youthful nursing work at Glamis during the war was testimony to her own sense of duty.

For whatever reasons, Elizabeth was clearly happy to receive Bertie's attentions and even to encourage them. In August 1920 they were both logged as being on board the King's yacht *Britannia* when she won the thirty-nine-mile premier race at Cowes. A month later the duke's name appears for the first time in the visitors' book at Glamis when he stayed at the castle between 18 and 20 September 1920. With the exception of David who was still on his world tour, the whole of the royal family were in residence at Balmoral for the shooting season. James Stuart and the duke managed to slip away briefly from the dullness of Balmoral's settled routines and predictable guest-lists to the obvious attractions of Glamis.

Their friend Michael Bowes Lyon was at home; James's brother, Lord Doune, was also staying, as were various pretty girls including Helen Cecil, Doris Gordon-Lennox and Katharine Hamilton. Bertie's sister Princess Mary was staying with Lady Airlie at nearby Cortachy, and she too came over for a day. It was a wonderfully lively and unconstrained party and Bertie must have been sad to leave, although the *Tatler* reported him soon after at shooting parties with the Earl of Pembroke and Sir Ernest Cassel. Such were the burdens of royalty. Possibly he would have preferred to have remained in Scotland for Lord Glamis's own shoot that October: the *Tatler* recorded that it was a great success and that both Elizabeth and James Stuart were of the party.

It did not escape the Queen's notice that her son talked constantly about Lady Elizabeth and by Christmas she decided to consult Mabell Airlie about the matter.

On a winter's afternoon drive, the Queen confided to Lady Airlie that Lloyd George had told the King that foreign brides for the two older princes would not be tolerated: they would have to find suitable matches among the British aristocracy. 'I don't think Bertie will be sorry to hear that,' she added. 'I have discovered that he is very much attracted to Lady Elizabeth Bowes Lyon. He's always talking about her. She seems a charming girl but I don't know her very well.'

This was Lady Airlie's cue. She retained a great affection for Bertie and was a lifelong friend of the Strathmores. She reassured the Queen that she had known the girl all her life 'and could say nothing but good of her'. It was understood that the lady-in-waiting was to act as go-between.

'Soon after that,' she relates, 'the duke and Lady Elizabeth started dropping in at my flat, on various pretexts, always separately but each talked of the other. She was frankly doubtful, uncertain of her feelings, and afraid of the public life which would lie ahead of her as the King's daughter-in-law. The duke's humility was touching. He was deeply in love.'

Bertie's eagerness was manifest. His prospective bride's hesitation, therefore, must have puzzled Queen Mary. She belonged to the generation which believed firmly that children, especially daughters, should do as they were told. Her son was a royal prince and obviously devoted to Elizabeth. Wasn't she at the very least fond of him? From the Queen's perspective it was unthinkable that Elizabeth should turn him down.

Encourged by his mother and prodded by his elder brother, Bertie came to a decision. In the spring of 1921 his proposal was put to Elizabeth. It was refused.

Lady Airlie wrote to Lady Strathmore that 'the Duke looked so disconsolate. I do hope he will find a nice wife who will make him happy.' Elizabeth's mother replied prophetically, 'I like him so much and he is a man who will be made or marred by his wife.'

CHAPTER TEN

Bertie, at last

· · · ⬥ · · ·

I T IS NOT surprising that Elizabeth turned down Bertie's first tentative proposal. Those who thought otherwise, including Queen Mary, had reckoned without her fierce independence and her determination to make the correct choice. 'Aunt Elizabeth had so many people desperate to marry her that she was going to take her time and make sure that her decision was the right one,' says Mary Clayton. 'What many people forget is that in those days you were heavily chaperoned wherever you went. It took longer to get to know people properly. You were never alone with a young man. Life was so much more formal then. It is not like nowadays when you go out with one person and there is a degree of intimacy.'

Early in 1921 there was nothing to suggest that Elizabeth was in love with Bertie, as he so transparently was with her. More significantly, James Stuart was still very much in evidence. That was inevitable: as the duke's equerry James went almost everywhere his master did.

The rejection must have been all the more distressing for Bertie as he watched his acquaintances pairing off. Elizabeth was a bridesmaid at the society wedding of Helen Cecil, who had been at Glamis the previous summer, to the King's private secretary Alec Hardinge. The ceremony took place at St Paul's, Knightsbridge. Arthur Penn was best man and the guest list included Diamond Hardinge, Doris Gordon-Lennox and Mollie Lascelles. Later in the year, it was Mollie's turn, when she married the Earl of Dalkeith, heir to the Duke of Buccleuch.

Bertie and Elizabeth remained good friends, meeting at Ascot and Henley as the season propelled them in and out of each other's company. August brought the annual exodus to Scotland – and an unexpected visitor. Queen Mary had decided to forgo her usual summer visit to the Grand Duchess of Mecklenburg-Strelitz and

The special wedding issue of the *Dundee Advertiser*, 24 April 1923.
The Mad Hatters were well represented among the bridesmaids

WINDSOR · GLAMIS

THE BRIDE AND BRIDEGROOM

H.M. The King

H.M. The Queen

Lady Mary Cambridge

Hon. Cecilia Bowes Lyon

Lady Katherine Hamilton

Lady May Cambridge

Lady Mary Thynne

Miss Betty Cator

Hon. Elizabeth Elphinstone

Hon. Diamond Hardinge

The Earl of Strathmore

The Countess of Strathmore

Lady Elizabeth's Message
Specially Written for the "Dundee Advertiser"

It would be impossible for me to make personal acknowledgement of all the kindly thoughts and good wishes conveyed to me in view of my approaching marriage, but my first word of thanks is naturally due to the people of Scotland, and particularly to the people of my own county of Forfarshire and of the city of Dundee.

My engagement has only occasioned an even warmer manifestation of that kindness which has always been shown to me during the whole of our association.

It is specially gratifying to me that all parts of the country have been represented in the messages of congratulation which have been received, but no greetings have been more welcome than those which come from Scotland, and the various associations there with which I have been connected.

In all that I have written, my feelings are fully shared by the Duke of York.

Elizabeth Bowes Lyon

headed north, to stay with Lady Airlie at Cortachy Castle. Her Majesty had an ulterior motive. Soon she was motoring down the road to visit Glamis.

Lady Strathmore had been ill for some time and so, as the two chauffeur-driven cars pulled up at the castle gates on 9 September, Lady Elizabeth was waiting on the steps to greet the royal guest. If she felt nervous she did not show it. She was relaxed and charming, giving the royal party a guided tour before sitting down to tea. The Queen, always interested in family histories, was impressed by the young woman's knowledge and still more by her manner. By the time she departed, she had decided that Lady Elizabeth was 'the one girl who could make Bertie happy'.

Bertie and the rest of that season's shooting party, including James Stuart and the younger Bowes Lyon brothers, arrived on 24 September and stayed for a week. Immediately they left, Lady Strathmore underwent a major operation. During this time of great anxiety for Elizabeth, Bertie was most sympathetic and kept in close touch with her. He had had an ulcer operated on in 1917 and well understood the anxiety attached to any operation. He tried to reassure Elizabeth and praised her for keeping up her spirits with such a threat hanging over the family.

By this time Bertie had grown fond of them all; he had become firm friends with Michael and David, and been touched by the unaffected kindness he had received at their home. His return to London and the loneliness of life at Buckingham Palace were now all the harder to bear. Time hung heavily on his hands, particularly between tea and dinner, when it was too dark to play tennis. Most of the people he knew were still away and there were no parties or distractions to relieve the ennui. He was longing for Elizabeth to come south again.

News that Lady Strathmore had come through the operation was greeted with delight by Prince Albert, although later complications meant that he continued to lend a sympathetic ear to her daughter's worries. As Elizabeth stayed in Scotland to nurse her mother through her convalescence, Bertie thoughtfully despatched the latest dance tunes to Glamis to cheer her up. He was proving a devoted friend. Undoubtedly his kindness and sympathy made an impression.

Meanwhile, James Stuart had left the Duke of York's service as his equerry and, as we have seen, was to leave the country too, bound for the oilfields of Oklahoma. This removed from the arena Bertie's only serious rival. James was at Glamis briefly over the New Year of 1922, to say goodbye. He was not to return until after Bertie and Elizabeth were married.

That January, whatever Princess Mary's private emotions, society was agog at the prospect of her forthcoming marriage to Viscount Lascelles. The *Tatler's* 'Letters from Evelyn' column reflected the excitement:

> What a difference Princess Mary's wedding is going to make to February when most of the social world who can afford it have generally flown to Egypt and the Riviera, Biarritz and the north of Africa. They tell me that the big hotels like Claridge's and the Ritz have been inundated already with inquiries for rooms, not only from the privileged two thousand who will be in the Abbey but from hundreds more as well who want to be on the spot.

As the hunt ball season reached its climax and the polo season opened in Cannes, the *Tatler* reported further news: among Princess Mary's bridesmaids would be 'the exquisite Lady Mary Thynne, Lady Rachel Cavendish and Lady Elizabeth Bowes Lyon, whose names have been so persistently rumoured as possible brides for the royal princes'.

The royal wedding galvanised society. There was a fashion for charity balls to raise money for war veterans, orphans and the disabled. There was also a sudden craze for mud baths, 'guaranteed to remove all the ravages made by our open-air life on the exposed parts of our bodies'.

In June, attendance at a royal wedding in Belgrade took Bertie even further from Elizabeth, and he showed little interest in yet another new rumour concerning his imminent betrothal – this time to Lady Mary Cambridge. By July, the prince was getting desperate and chose to unburden himself to the Prime Minister's Parliamentary Private Secretary, John Colin Campbell Davidson. The thirty-three-year-old Scottish MP was accosted by Louis Greig as he was about to leave for a ceremony commemorating the Dover Patrol at Dunkirk. He was then hustled aboard the destroyer *Versatile*, where Prince Albert was waiting in the wardroom. Once they were left alone, Bertie began to talk. Writing about this curious incident some thirty years later, Davidson recalled:

> I had not been in the duke's presence more than a few minutes before I realised that he was not only worried but genuinely unhappy. He seemed to have reached a crisis in his life, and wanted someone to whom he could unburden himself without reserve. He dwelt upon the difficulties which surrounded a King's son in contrast with men like myself who had always had greater freedom at school and university to make their own friends and a wider circle to choose from. We discussed friendship, and the relative value of brains and character, and all the sort of things that young

men do talk about in the abstract when in reality they are very much concerned in the concrete.

He told me that sometimes the discipline of the formality of the court proved irksome, and I sensed that he was working up to something important. I felt moved with a great desire to help him if I could, he was so simple, frank and forthcoming.

Then out it came. He declared that he was desperately in love, but that he was in despair for it seemed quite certain that he had lost the only woman he would ever marry. I told him that however black it looked, he must not give up hope; that my wife had refused me consistently before she finally said 'yes', and that like him, if she had persisted in her refusal, I would never have married anyone else.

Bertie went on to explain that, as the King's son, he could not propose himself because the strict rules of the court dictated that he could not put himself in a position to be refused. An emissary had already been sent to see if the girl would marry him and the answer had been 'No'. What should he do?

Davidson was in no doubt: 'I suggested that in the Year of Grace 1922 no high-spirited girl of character was likely to accept a proposal made at second hand; if she was fond of him as he thought she was, he must propose to her himself.'

Two months later Bertie was again invited to shoot at Glamis. 'Evelyn' of the *Tatler* was quick to comment: 'I wonder we have been spared the usual hints and rumours about Lord and Lady Strathmore's party, where the Duke of York, Prince Paul of Serbia, Lady Elizabeth Bowes Lyon, Lady Rachel Cavendish and her cousin, Miss Mary Cavendish, and Lady Doris Gordon-Lennox will all be up at Glamis together.'

Bertie still hoped to win Elizabeth. Some biographers have suggested that his persistent wooing was irritating her (at one point rumours were circulating of as many as seventeen failed proposals!), yet a very different picture is painted by the diarist Chips Channon, who was also staying at Glamis. 'One rainy afternoon, we were sitting about and I pretended I could read cards, and I told Elizabeth Lyon's fortune and predicted a great and glamorous royal future. She laughed, for it was obvious that the Duke of York was much in love with her.'

In December 1922 the whole country was excited by the news that Lord Carnarvon and Howard Carter had discovered the tomb of Tutankhamen. The *Tatler* was almost as thrilled by its own discovery that the Duke of York had dined *chez* the Ronald Grevilles in the company of Lady Elizabeth Bowes Lyon 'in silver tissue'.

184

As bridesmaid to the Princess
Royal, 28 February 1922.
The pair used to dance to
gramophone records at
Buckingham Palace

The *Tatler*, October 1921.
The shooting-party in full.
Back row: Michael, David,
Bertie, Lord Strathmore,
'Wisp' Leveson-Gower,
James. Front row: Doris
Gordon-Lennox, Mida Scott,
Elizabeth, Katharine
Hamilton, Rose

After dinner in the drawing-
room of Glamis Castle,
September 1922. Bertie had
just asked permission from
Lord Strathmore to propose.
It was to be four months
before she accepted him

OPPOSITE: A grinning Bertie
with Lady Strathmore. The
butler, Barson, stands in the
background

The following January, Elizabeth was staying with another of her admirers, George Gage, at his Tudor mansion in Sussex, when the *Daily News* claimed that the Prince of Wales was about to announce his engagement to a noble Scottish lady. The report left few in doubt as to her identity. However, the newspapers had the right story but the wrong prince. Lady Elizabeth was not amused. As Chips Channon recorded the occasion:

> The evening papers have announced her engagement to the Prince of Wales. So we all bowed and bobbed and teased her, calling her 'Ma'am': I am not sure that she enjoyed it. It couldn't be true, but how delighted everyone would be! She certainly has something on her mind. She is more gentle, lovely and exquisite than any woman alive, but this evening I thought her unhappy and distraite. I longed to tell her I would die for her, although I am not in love with her.

Eight days later Bertie was walking with her in the woods at St Paul's Walden Bury when he proposed once more, but this time in person. Elizabeth accepted him and the duke was overjoyed. He sent a pre-arranged telegram to his parents at Sandringham saying simply 'All right, Bertie.'

Congratulations flooded in. Elizabeth told her friends how pleased she was to be engaged. The only problem was the press attention, which she loathed. Undaunted, 'Evelyn' of the *Tatler* (which had a portrait of the happy couple on its cover) reported breathlessly:

> Aren't you thrilled and glad that the royal engagement is announced at last? Of course it has been rumoured and talked about for the last eighteen months or more, but nobody seemed quite to know whether it would or would not come off. Probably the two didn't know themselves. It is a big position with big responsibilities for a young girl who isn't of royal blood to have to face.

The Bowes Lyons' old friend Freddie Dalrymple-Hamilton turned once more to his diary: 'Elizabeth is going to marry the Duke of York and it was in all the papers this morning. I will write to her and Lady Strathmore. I do hope it'll be the greatest success in every way and he is a very fortunate bloke, Duke of York or not!'

Perhaps it is to Freddie's unpublished account rather than to any of the newspaper reports that we should turn for the events that followed. He and his wife Gwendoline were guests at a private party given three days before the wedding, which was to be on 26 April 1923. 'Gwen and I went to the evening party at Buckingham Palace and it was very amusing,' he recorded.

We bowed to the King and Queen and then to Elizabeth and the Duke of York. Elizabeth was splendid and looked lovely and seemed to take everything very calmly as I never had any doubt she would.

We got there pretty early and had no trouble at all. Saw all the rest of the family there also and a certain amount of others we knew. Inspected the presents some of which were gorgeous and I wish I could have removed a few ... I didn't manage to talk to Elizabeth but we had to content ourselves with making ugly faces at each other across the room.

Freddie was also at Westminster Abbey to see his friends united in holy matrimony by the Archbishops of Canterbury and York.

It started the day by streaming with rain but it improved later on. G. and I set forth for Westminster Abbey dressed in our best at 9.45 and were in our places by 10.15. We had very good places on the right of the aisle, close to the screen and about three rows from the front and had a first class view of the various processions. It actually was a most wonderful spectacle and most impressive.

All the most distinguished Admirals and Generals seemed to be just opposite and my humble rank seemed very inept in such a galaxy of glory!!

The organ, of course, was wonderful and so later was the singing. The royal procession started about 11.30, the Queen being a magnificent spectacle in a blue and silver dress and covered with jewels etc. The Duke of York came up between the Prince of Wales and Prince Harry with Louis Greig heading his procession. We managed to catch his eye as he passed or thought we did as he half grimaced at us. I must ask some day!

The organ which had been crashing loudly for some time suddenly lurched into 'Lead Us Heavenly Father, Lead Us' very softly which gave a most wonderful effect I thought and there was Elizabeth with her father and looking extraordinarily nice and I can't help feeling most extraordinarily proud of her as if she'd been my own sister.

She did it amazingly well and soon appeared to be enjoying it as she sailed up at Lord Strathmore's side, when he bent down and asked her something. Once they had passed the screen, we didn't see any more till they came back but we could hear all that was going on.

We had a good laugh at Elizabeth when she was coming back having got it over and she saw us and laughed too. After it was all over we were very lucky getting away and found our car almost at the door. Drove home and got out of our best clothes and then made our way on the top of a bus to the Ritz for lunch. Later G. and I went to see the Duke and Duchess of York start on their honeymoon and had a good view by Queen Victoria's memorial. She seemed very happy and so did he. There were large crowds to see the procession and they got an ovation.

We dined at the Guards' Club and drank their health.

The only slight hitch during the whole of her wedding day went unseen. According to Mabel Monty, in the heat of the moment the

The wedding issue of the
Dundee Advertiser. The
photograph of Elizabeth was
the duke's favourite

191

Leaving Bruton Street for
the Abbey

1923

CUPID

Elizabeth   May 8th ——— 17th

Albert   May 8th ——— 17th

Michael Lyon   June 2nd ——— 22nd

Joanne   August 14 ——— 4

Bruce Ogilvie   Aug. 17 ——— 21st

Lower Cavendish-Bentinck   Aug 24th ——— 29th

Betty Cavendish Bentinck   Aug. 24th ——— Sept. 3rd

Alice Cavendish Bentinck   "   "   "   "

Nina Balfour   Sep 1.   4

Archie Balfour   "   "   "   " bride left her gloves lying on the hall table of 17 Bruton Street. They were spotted just after her carriage had set off and a footman had to fight his way through the crowds to beat her to the Abbey. He arrived panting, in the nick of time, and managed to hand them to her bridesmaids just before she set off up the aisle.

It would never have done for the future Duchess of York and Queen of England to be married with ungloved hands.

From the visitors' book at Glamis, signed by Elizabeth and Bertie on their honeymoon. Note brother Michael's graphic comments

Envoi

· · · ⬥━━❦━━⬥ · · ·

LADY ELIZABETH arrived at Westminster Abbey a commoner, driven in a landau. She departed a duchess in a fairytale coach, heading a procession which included the King, two queens, numerous princes and princesses and the nation's most powerful politicians. After the journey through cheering jubilant crowds to Buckingham Palace and the obligatory balcony appearance, a magnificent wedding breakfast awaited the bride and groom, with dishes created especially for the occasion including Côtelette d'Agneau Prince Albert, Chapons à la Strathmore and Fraises Duchesse Elizabeth.

For Elizabeth, the whole affair must have been considerably more nerve-racking than the high-spirited society wedding of her girlhood dreams. The official group photographs show dispiritingly solemn faces. Only one shot gives a glimpse of the joy expected of a twenty-two-year-old on her wedding day: the famous picture of the Duke and Duchess of York leaving the palace courtyard in an open carriage en route for their honeymoon at Polesden Lacey. Elizabeth is tilting her smiling face up to the crowd of waving courtiers, while Bertie is being showered with rose petals. As an image it marks the end of her care-free youth: a farewell grin from the young woman once nicknamed Merry Mischief.

Within a few months of that day, 26 April 1923, the two young men who had been most prominent in her life until she accepted the prince's proposal were themselves married. The wedding of James Stuart and Lady Rachel Cavendish took place on 4 August 1923, Elizabeth's twenty-third birthday. The following October, Prince Paul of Serbia married Princess Olga of Greece at a grand ceremony in Belgrade. The Duke and Duchess of York were among the royal guests.

197

Despite her parents' distrust of life at court, Elizabeth's upbringing proved an excellent preparation for it. The most important factors were her mother's piety and sense of duty which determined the countess's own behaviour and greatly influenced that of her children. The young Elizabeth was full of fun and mischief yet she was no rebel. Her teenage flirtatiousness and love of parties were accompanied by an unquestioning sense of propriety and good behaviour. Above all, the experience of growing up in an enormous family, whose numbers were constantly swollen by visitors, gave her the ability to get on effortlessly with other people, whatever their age or station in life.

She was, in short, highly accomplished and experienced in the social conventions of the time, and onlookers at court were soon admiring her 'serene professionalism'. Her father-in-law, King George V, had recognised her qualities even earlier. 'I am quite certain,' he wrote to Bertie during the honeymoon, 'that Elizabeth will be a splendid partner in your work and share with you and help you in all you have to do.' The King had already confided to his second son his anxieties about the Prince of Wales, so these words carried some significance. Years later, a lady-in-waiting overheard the King's even more outspoken comments: 'I pray to God that my eldest son will never marry and have children, and that nothing will come between Bertie and Lillibet and the throne.'

Nothing did; but it was a near thing. The story of the Queen Mother's life repeatedly invites the question 'What if?' What if Queen Mary had succeeded in propelling Bertie into marriage before the Farquhars' ball in May 1920? What if Mrs Simpson had not so captivated David that he chose her before his throne? Above all, what if Elizabeth as the debutante of the day had followed the inclinations of her heart? What if she had allowed herself to be wooed and won by the man who, as we have now been told, was the love of her young life? Elizabeth hesitated for nearly two years before accepting Bertie's offer of marriage. She was fond of him, that was plain. But something, or someone, stopped her from saying yes. Was it her reluctance to take on the responsibilities of royalty, as most biographers imply? Or was there more to it than that?

The twenty-one-year old Elizabeth could have had her pick of half a dozen serious suitors. One of them, James Stuart, was particularly favoured. It seems beyond doubt that she was in love with him. Two incidents suggest that his presence was part of Bertie's problem: the first was James's sudden resignation as the prince's equerry in 1921; the second was his precipitate departure to work in the Oklahoma oilfields a few months later. Were these events merely coincidental?

Or were they, as seems more than probable, the result of a conspiracy devised by Queen Mary to remove the prince's rival from the scene? If so, the plan worked, and posterity has cause to be grateful.

Elizabeth may have taken a long time to choose but the decision was hers alone and, as her niece points out, that was a measure of how seriously she took marriage. She waited because she had to be sure that Bertie was the right man for her and that she could make him happy. What then were the qualities that made Elizabeth accept Bertie?

Firstly, she recognised in him an inner strength which was to lead his father to admit that, of all his children, 'Bertie had more guts than the rest of them put together.'

Also, like Elizabeth, Bertie had the keen sense of duty and desire 'to be of use' that had been instilled in his future wife from childhood. She respected the fact that, despite his speech impediment, he overcame his anxiety at public speaking in order to carry out a full load of official engagements.

The opinion of her family would have weighed heavily in the balance when Elizabeth considered her future and, although the Strathmores traditionally had a dislike of court life, they approved the match and thought it would lead to a happy and successful marriage.

Above all, Bertie was clearly devoted to her and his kind heart was never more in evidence than at the time of her mother's illness when she was sustained by his unfailing love and thoughtfulness.

Finally, she realised that Bertie needed her, the country needed her and, as she told a friend at the time, she 'couldn't live without him'. As she wrote to her closest confidantes, she had surprised even herself by taking the plunge but, once she had done so, she felt incredibly happy. When her future husband telegraphed his parents with the message, 'All right, Bertie,' it was no more than the truth. They were to make a matchless team both on and off duty and, as The Queen Mother once famously remarked when praised for her efforts, 'It was not me. We did it together.'

Illustration credits

· · · ⟨✦⟩ · · ·

The illustrations for *My Darling Buffy* come almost exclusively from private collections and I owe a special debt of gratitude to the Earl of Strathmore and Kinghorne, HRH Prince Alexander of Yugoslavia, Lady Mary Clayton, le Comte de Ribes, Viscount Gage, Viscount Stuart of Findhorn, Lady Penn, the Hon. Mrs Ritchie, Mrs Cynthia Munro and Mrs Mabel Stringer.

Other illustrations were supplied by:

Camera Press, Photograph by ILN: 192
Camera Press, Photograph by Bassano: Back Endpaper
Dundee Advertiser: 179, 190, 191
Hulton Deutsch Collection: 86, 175
Hulton Getty Picture Collection: 52

Index

203

206